THE TOTAL RUNNER:

A Complete Mind-Body Guide to Optimal Performance

THE TOTAL RUNNER:

A Complete Mind-Body Guide to Optimal Performance

Dr. Jerry Lynch

Illustrations by Dobbin von Puck

PRENTICE-HALL, INC./Englewood Cliffs, New Jersey

Prentice-Hall International, Inc., *London*
Prentice-Hall of Australia, Pty. Ltd., *Sydney*
Prentice-Hall Canada, Inc., *Toronto*
Prentice-Hall of India Private Ltd., *New Delhi*
Prentice-Hall of Japan, Inc., *Tokyo*
Prentice-Hall of Southeast Asia Pte. Ltd., *Singapore*
Whitehall Books, Ltd., Wellington, *New Zealand*
Editora Prentice-Hall do Brasil Ltda., *Rio de Janeiro*
Prentice-Hall Hispanoamericana, S.A., *Mexico*

© 1987 *by*
Dr. Jerry Lynch

Library of Congress Cataloging-in-Publication Data

Lynch, Jerry
  The total runner.

  Includes index.
  1. Running — Psychological aspects.   2. Mind and body.
I. Title.
GV1061.8.P75L86   1986   796.4'26   86-16913

0-13-925678-4

0-13-925660-1 {PBK}

Printed in the United States of America

Introduction

Perhaps one of the most exciting and rewarding aspects to life is the experience of going beyond what were once thought to be limitations. We begin to realize that many of our limiting beliefs about what can or cannot be done are simply preconceived restrictions and attitudes taught to us by parents, teachers, friends, and others during our formative years, with no objective basis for reality. The most damaging of these beliefs, is the notion that such "restrictions" are etched in stone, never to be changed; to be accepted as a blueprint for our future without question. As I began to experience life, I slowly realized that many of these "accepted truisms" were, indeed, unidimensional limitations that I might be able to transcend. Rather than accept what was, I began to dream how things could be better and asked "why not?" With that question as a modus operandi for everyday living, I began to experience incredible breakthroughs into territories that I once feared to tread. My beliefs about what was now possible became quite expansive. Since most people rarely utilize more than 10 percent of their physical and mental capabilities, I knew that I probably couldn't imagine where my real limits reside. Excited about this vast potential, I became totally committed to the goal of sharing this personal "discovery" with all of you who have the dream of self-expansion; thus, the reason for this book.

Written through the medium of the sport of running, it will facilitate movement toward higher levels of personal excellence in all areas of performance.

The book begins with a thorough explanation of how the body and mind work harmoniously to facilitate optimal performance. In Chapter 1 you will learn how elite athletes use their mind to achieve excellence. A self-assessment test will help you to measure your strengths and weaknesses in the area of mental fitness and in so doing will enable you to decide which of the subsequent chapters will be most important to you, personally.

Chapters 2 and 3 are the foundations for all aspects of mental training. Peak performance begins with relaxation and inner control; practical techniques for achieving relaxation are offered in Chapter 2. Once relaxed, Chapter 3 will help you to understand the most widely used techniques of visualization, and how to apply it to all endeavors. The importance of this concept has been discovered by successful people throughout the world. It is the single most important ingredient you can use to improve any performance.

Are you not achieving your goals in life? Perhaps you are not committed, although you think you are. Chapter 4 will help you to know if there is true commitment on your part. A commitment rating scale is also included to assess your level as well as ways to develop a stronger commitment.

Most of us do not achieve our goals because we simply do not know how to establish them. If goals are too unrealistic or not specifically defined, you may be continually frustrated and disappointed only to give up your dreams. Learn how to set personalized plans for progress and insure the chances of reaching them in Chapter 5. You can get what you want if you just know how to go about setting goals.

Are you afraid of failure or success? Do you "burn-out" often and search for ways to become motivated? Do you struggle with seeing yourself as an athlete or optimal performer due to a low self-image? Are you constantly getting injured and wonder how to change that pattern? Does your mind wander during an event making it difficult, if not impossible, to regain concentration? This book will help you to overcome these obstacles by offering you ways to understand why they occur as well as practical strategies and techniques to use in gaining greater control over them.

Competitive pressure is a universal albatross for many performers. It creates behavior that impedes progress and blocks the path to success. In Chapter 10, you will learn how to "deflate" such pressure by using the Triple-A Procedure as well as understanding the 11 basic attitudes that hinder performance.

Many athletes ask how to achieve their "mental best" the day of the event. Chapter 11 will help to improve the chances for such an occurrence through the process of "competitive psychling," a countdown program beginning two weeks prior to the event. In addition, information on how to regulate the mental component during and after the contest will be thoroughly discussed. Post-event concerns, whether they be the thrill of victory or the agony of defeat, require one's mental attention if performance is to improve in the future.

Since our language creates images, and since we perform according to these images 90% of the time, it behooves us to regulate the constant negative messages that we may create in our minds. Statements such as "I can't . . .," "I'll never . . ." or "I am awkward" could preclude our taking action that would allow us to change. Chapter 13 will provide strategies to help you change any negative words and images that hinder your performance.

Finally, peak experience is something we have heard about; many of us have firsthand knowledge of "going beyond" during our athletic careers. Chapter 14 will take a close look into this phenomenon by relating true life experiences of famous world class athletes as well as those of the universal recreational enthusiast. It can happen to you and when it does, you'll want to enjoy it thoroughly. This segment will help you to do so.

The mental strategies, techniques, and exercises within these pages, are adaptable to all arenas of performance: the corporate executive, the athlete, the musician, the dancer, the teacher, or partners in a relationship; all performers and achievers will increase their chances of excellence by incorporating the ideas from this book into their lives.

As a former coach, a current nationally competitive runner, and a sports psychologist, I bring to this book a unique perspective on excellence and performance. Psychologists have been accused of being "lab buffs" content to experiment in the security of their "halls of ivy" refusing to "dirty their hands on the field of play." I write from personal experience as well as my years of work with athletes in individual and group situations. I love working "in the trenches" where the action is, and by so doing, I have narrowed the gap that so many feel exists between the university laboratory and the sports community.

The mental component of performance, always recognized as important, is now beginning to get the attention it deserves. Professional and Olympic athletes are employing the services of sports psychologists to help maximize performance. While conducting seminars at the U.S. Olympic Training Center (U.S.O.T.C.) in Colorado, I always ask the elite athletes what percentage of their performance on any given day is attributed to their level of mental fitness. Invariably, they state that it is 80-90 percent; being mentally prepared is crucial and cannot be overlooked if you want to be a complete athlete. We have devoted an enormous amount of energy to the development of muscle strength, proper diet, endurance, race strategy and coordination for the purposes of improvement. As we begin to level out with our performance, the need to develop the mind becomes even more important. The major breakthroughs in sporting events will now be reserved for those who train the mind on a regular basis. The book will help you to become your own "head" coach in order to be at the forefront of your chosen event.

Jerry Lynch

ACKNOWLEDGEMENTS

Optimal performance and effort is rarely possible without the support and encouragement of significant others. I wish to extend sincere gratitude and appreciation to the following people who helped make this book a reality.

- First, to all those athletes and performers who taught me much of what I know about human performance.

- To my friend, Sally Vance, who unselfishly gave of her time to the typing of this manuscript.

- To my friend, Dobbin von Puck, whose talent is clearly evident in his illustrations throughout this book; he never gave up on this project.

- And, of course, to my best friend and wife, Jan, whose goal throughout this project was to support and facilitate my growth as a writer. She gave so much of her time to give me a chance to realize my potential.

- Finally, to Tom Power, editor at Prentice-Hall, who recognized the potential in my manuscript and gave me the chance to carry out this dream.

J.L.

Contents

THE TOTAL RUNNER:

A Complete Mind-Body Guide to Optimal Performance

1

Compared to what we ought to be, we are only one-half awaken. We are making use of only a small part of our physical and mental resources . . . the human individual thus lives far within his (her) limits . . . and possesses power of various sorts which (s)he habitually fails to use.

William James (philosopher)

Hitching the Mental Horse to the Physical Wagon: The Mind-Body Athlete

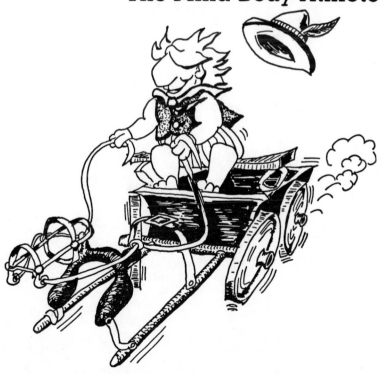

All of us athletes, elite and recreational alike, would like to experience at some point in time that seemingly evasive *super-performance* when the body and mind work in harmony to bring out our best. Perhaps this is why you have decided to read this book; you are looking for a guide to facilitate this process. I think you have taken a very important step in that direction.

What we athletes are disturbingly discovering is that there is a limit to the amount of training we can do before injury and/or mental-physical fatigue occur. There is just so much time in the day available for workouts, weight training, stretching and racing. Since we can't push these aspects of our development any further, we are now pursuing the "new horizon" of performance—the MIND. Although relatively new for us, the mind-body connection and its importance in sport has been acknowledged for hundreds of years throughout the world. The Greeks, as far back as 884 B.C., recognized the importance of creating harmony between the body and mind; training the mind, for them, was as important as developing the body. At the turn of this century (1917), the Soviet Union began to place a high premium on the importance of the mind for optimal performance. The first American to research the mental aspects to sport was Coleman Griffith during the 1920's at the University of Illinois. Recognized as "the Father of Sports Psychology," Coleman published a number of books on the subject, including his classic *Psychology and Athletics*. His work had been virtually ignored by coaches in this country until the mid-1960's as a reaction to the Soviets' and Eastern bloc nations' use of psychologists on their national teams during the 1952 Olympics. The concern over the mind-body connection, asleep for over 50 years in the U.S.A., is beginning to come alive as we try to regain our lost pre-eminence in world athletic competition—a place yielded to the Soviets and their satellite countries over the last two decades. Iron curtain countries have been winning medals in sports considered traditionally American. We are probably a good 10 years behind, but quickly closing the gap. To have watched the winter and summer Olympics of 1984 was to see the enormous interest displayed by American athletes with respect to the value of sports psychologists as adjuncts to their training and performance. Statements like ''the mind makes the difference between winning and losing'' were often verbalized by the elite during TV coverage of the games and other national media. Terms such as concentration, momentum, desire, commitment, fear of failure, psych-up, and pscyh-out are now the familiar lexicon of the mind-body athlete.

Although many of our national sports organizations have lagged behind this vital arena to excellence, the athletes, nevertheless, have searched for ways to improve performance through mental preparation; they know its importance, yet, for the most part, remain frustrated over the paucity of resources available. Slowly but surely, help is being provided.

From my experience with athletes at the U.S. Olympic Training Center, I can report that leadership in the application of psychological principles and strategies are beginning to be provided to our elite athletes. I see a growing concern in my private practice for such strategies with recreational athletes as well.

How much importance do athletes attach to the role of the mind in super-performance and excellence in sport? Gold medal decathlete, Bruce Jenner, has stated that Olympic competition is 80 percent mental challenge and 20 percent physical. To him, it becomes a question of getting your well-trained body to do its thing at a precise moment given all the confounding variables. Each year at the U.S. Olympic Training Center, I ask a new group of elite marathoners, ''What percentage of your performance on a given day can be attributed to your mental preparedness?'' The answers invariably fall between 85 to 90 percent. World class runner Marty Liquori once claimed that the most important component to his training regimen was his mental preparation.

One of the more widely used psychological techniques for producing excellence in running is the use of visualization or mental imagery (See Chapter 3 on visualization). America's premier miler, Steve Scott, uses this technique to rehearse important races. Prior to the 1979 AAU Championships, where he ran against Don Paige in the 1500-meter event, he visualized for two weeks, "where I would be in every stage of the race . . . racing completely relaxed, I heard the splits I wanted to hear and pictured the exact point I would overtake Paige . . . the race came out exactly as I had visualized it—right down to the splits."

Roger Bannister, one-time British world class miler, imagined in his mind the entire race scenario prior to his shattering of the four-minute barrier. He visualized the process of victory and refused to accept the images of others and their beliefs about how impossible it would be to run a four-minute mile. Anyone who watched the 1984 Olympic high jump competition remembers Dwight Stones and his intense concentration. He seemed to visualize "externally" as his head pointed to each step, and his arms and legs moved as if the jump were taking place. He saw in his mind the entire approach and take-off. He may do this two or three times before his actual jump. Although he didn't win the Gold, his performance was, indeed, optimal.

Elite athlete, Tony Sandoval, told me that he visualized the entire 1980 Olympic marathon trials prior to his victory. He heard splits, saw surges and other important facets of the run in explicit detail.

Lee Evans, 1968 Olympic gold medalist in the 400-meter event, mentally prepared each stride of his performance for two full years before the event took place. He ran one of the most brilliant 400-meter races in Olympic history, clocking 43.86, a world record that still remains.

Herb Lindsay, premier American road racer in 1980-81, is a firm believer in the power of the mind. While accompanying Herb on one of his easy training runs in the foothills of Boulder, Colorado, I observed his ritual of solitude for five minutes after a run. During that time, he mentally rehearses his "feeling"—one of gliding, effortless motion—and captures it for future reference while racing. Herb is the epitome of the renaissance athlete.

Jon Sinclair, Dick Beardsley, Dean Matthews—the list of runners goes on and on. As I work with these fantastic athletes, I learn so much about the effect of the mind on performance. They never fail to reinforce what I already believe—that limits are barriers that we manufacture for our unconscious convenience. Our limits are illusions for the most part. The greatness of the African runners could be attributed to the fact that they have no illusions about not being able to run any faster. They regard no pace as too fast. This explains, in part, the quadruple world record performance by Kenyan Henry Rono. According to world class runner Kenny Moore, Rono has no illusions to hold him back; he regards no record as unbreakable.

If the foregoing examples demonstrate anything, it is that we runners and other athletes must not impose barriers or limits on what is possible. We can and will begin to transcend our limits and go beyond the confines of our anatomical structures when we learn how to "tune-in" to the powers of the mind. It is important to understand that the mind cannot help you to overcome your *REAL limitations*; it does, however, allow you to go beyond what you *THINK* are your limits. These latter barriers fall exponentially short of those real limitations; there's an incredible amount of room for growth, change and development.

Examples of people going beyond what they think are limits are widespread. How many of us could imagine a 65-pound nine-year-old lifting a car? Jeremy Schill, from North Dakota, accomplished this feat when he rescued his dad from under a 2-ton car that had crashed down on him when the jack slipped. There is no logical explanation for Jeremy's heroic act in physical terms alone. The influence of the psychological on such performance must be given credence.

John Jerome, in his book *The Sweet Spot in Time*, addresses the influence of mental aspects upon optimal performance in sport. The most outrageous example of going beyond "limits" in track and field is the super-performance by long jumper Bob Beamon during the 1968 Olympics in Mexico City. His extraordinary jump of 29 feet 2 1/2 inches was a full 2 feet farther than the world record. Most track experts feel that this feat would be equivalent to lowering the world record in the mile to 3:25 in one race. Marathoners would have to lower the world record to under two hours, a feat that most top runners would say is inconceivable. Yet both of those events, the mile and marathon, will reach those levels of performance. After all, prior to Roger Bannister's breaking of the four-minute barrier in the mile, over 50 reputable medical journals throughout the world claimed that such speed by a human was not only impossible, but unthinkable. Once Bannister transcended that "limit," the sub-four-minute mile became commonplace as over 50 athletes mimicked his performance over the next year and one half. I find it hard to believe that all those runners magically became so fast within that time frame. A more likely explanation is that once the barrier was lifted, they could mentally "see" that it was possible. The illusion of the impossibility of running under four minutes was shattered—and illusions are the figments of the imagination, perceptions of the mind.

John Lilly, dolphin research psychologist, once said, "Beliefs are limits to be examined and transcended." If you have ever believed that you could accomplish a certain task, you probably could; when you believed you couldn't, you were probably correct. When have you ever not accomplished something that you knew you could and wanted to at the same time? Have you ever had pre-conceived ideas about limitations, only to go beyond and realize that you are capable of so much more than once imagined? Researcher Dr. George Lozanov has stated that "we are conditioned to believe that we can only learn so much so fast, that we are bound to be sick, that there are certain rigid limits to what we can do and achieve, and we are bombarded constantly with limiting suggestions . . . belief in limits creates limited people . . . both history and experimental data show that humans possess vastly larger capabilities than those they now use." According to author Dr. Jean Houston, "we are just beginning to discover the virtually *unlimited* capacities of the mind." From my experiences, it appears that we cannot come close to imagining our greatest potentials. I can see no limits (although ultimately they may be there). If you question this statement, I must ask you if you truly feel that you have ever pushed out far enough to find out if those limits exist. There always seems to be more than you can be or do. Karl Mohr, talent developer and optimal specialist for the University of California Swim Team at Berkeley, sums up my feelings: "Don't limit yourself in any way. Let go of the past. Get off your position (beliefs). Give yourself the space to become everything that you are capable of being. You are the only one that can fulfill your imagined potential.'' If there are limits to what we can do, I can't see them.

When I talk with runners, they seem to be well-educated with regard to their physical training and what needs to be done to get the body in shape. The *mind*, however, is "new turf" and presents a formidable challenge; they realize how important the mental domain is to performance, yet the road to developing this arena is elusive at best. This book is written to help facilitate the development of your *mental game*; but for now, let's take a look at the major areas of concern that you, the mind-body athlete, may have. For example, do you need to develop strategies and techniques in the area of relaxation and visualization? Are you truly committed to your sport, and how can you measure that? What about the process of goal-setting? Do you have a workable mental game plan prior to and during a race? Do you lose motivation easily? Is your self-image interfering with optimal performance? Is concentration an elusive entity for you? Do the fears of failure and/or success stand in your way? Are you injury prone and seem unable to change the pattern? These and many other questions are issues frequently brought to my attention by athletes. These personal concerns will be addressed when you take the *Runner's Mental Fitness Test*; it should help to clarify those areas needing work and refer you to those chapters that specifically discuss those personal issues. All of the chapters in the book will, hopefully, shed varying degrees of light upon this exciting area of athletic training.

The items in this test represent the *key* factors to be included in a sound mental training program. Sometimes one area may be handled in two or more chapters. For the best results, remember that there are no right or wrong answers. Respond as if no one but yourself will read the score. Let this be a positive experience which indicates to you the areas of mental preparation needing the most work. Evaluate the results rather than rationalize them. The latter approach leads you down the road of stagnation. Any response of 1, 2 or 3 should warrant your attention, with the lowest score being the most crucial and immediate of concerns.

> *SCORING SYSTEM:* For all Statements
>
> | Never | – 1 | Often | – 4 |
> | Seldom | – 2 | Always | – 5 |
> | Sometimes | – 3 | | |

RUNNER'S MENTAL FITNESS TEST

3   1. I find it easy to get "psyched-up" for a race. (Chapters 3 and 1)

2   2. I become totally focused and absorbed in a race. (Chapters 3 and 12)

3   3. I am very confident that I will do well in competition. (Chapters 3, 7, 8, 10, 11, and 12)

3   4. I have a clear, positive image of self as a runner. (Chapter 8)

2   5. My running goals are realistic, challenging, and specifically defined. (Chapter 5)

3   6. When tired, I can usually motivate myself to go for a run. (Chapter 6)

3   7. I feel more committed to running improvement than anything else. (Chapter 4)

3   8. I mentally rehearse (visualize) my race performance prior to its occurrence. (Chapters 2 and 3)

2   9. Specific relaxation techniques are often used in conjunction with my visualization. (Chapter 2)

2   10. Fatigue is an entity that I view as mostly mental and able to be controlled. (Chapter 3)

3   11. When I make a tactical error while racing, I can mentally recover and concentrate. (Chapters 3, 11, and 12)

3   12. Prior to a race, I can stay calm if I so desire. (Chapters 2, 3, and 11)

7   13. I concentrate more on *my* race strategies, rather than my competitors'. (Chapter 10)

3   14. I often think about setting *Personal Bests*. (Chapter 3)

4   15. Prior to a race, I imagine how good I'll feel during and after the event. (Chapters 3 and 11)

16. I often dream about being successful and reaching my goals. (Chapter 3)

17. I can usually avoid becoming too tense during a competitive event. (Chapter 11)

18. I usually can "go for it" during a race without the fear of failing. (Chapter 7)

19. Poor performances are usually viewed as a learning situation for future improvement. (Chapter 7)

20. I frequently imagine my training runs being successful prior to their occurrence. (Chapter 3)

21. I find that I can control my level of arousal prior to a race. (Chapter 11)

22. Adverse conditions, such as inclement weather or hills, give me a psychological advantage during competition. (Chapters 3 and 11)

23. My self-confidence remains intact regardless of who shows up for a race. (Chapters 3, 8, and 10)

24. I can mentally "see" myself as a smooth, efficient, capable runner. (Chapter 3)

25. I try to remember my successful experiences rather than my past failures. (Chapters 3, 7, 8, and 13)

How You Scored

If you scored 43 points or less: POOR MENTAL FITNESS

You've got a long way to go. Shoes and intuition have gotten you this far but are not enough to allow for breakthroughs. You are a runner who rarely works on the connection between mental training and performance, if at all. On a positive note, you are now *aware* of the many factors involved in training the mind for optimal performance. You were looking for ways to improve and if you devote some of your time to the mental aspects of training, predictably, you will improve rapidly.

If you scored 44-67 points: MARGINAL MENTAL FITNESS

You are a runner who is sporadically aware of the mind-body connection. You probably experience mental sluggishness at times and feel frustrated by your lack of progress for all the work you do.

You probably believe that mentally tough athletes are born that way; you've either got it or you don't. Good news for you: being mentally strong is a learned behavior. The more you practice with the mind, the easier it becomes and the better you will get. You can start your program by learning how to relax the mind while using exercises in visual imagery. "See" yourself perform as you so desire.

If you scored 68-89 points: AVERAGE MENTAL FITNESS

You definitely see a strong connection between your mental preparation and performance. You notice how well you race when the body and mind are partners. Your inconsistency in performance is traceable to the times when you are not mentally there, assuming the physical work has been done. You probably search out information on the topic only to realize that not much is available on the bookshelves. You need to become more consistent with what you do on your good days. Try to locate someone to help you get started or write to me and I'll help you where I can.

If you scored 90-104: ABOVE AVERAGE MENTAL FITNESS

You are probably running very well whether you are competing or not; competitively, you are perhaps in the top of your age group locally. (Others with less mental fitness may perform better by overcompensating on the physical end—if they would use the mind, their optimal performance would be enhanced exponentially). If you check your responses to the staements, you may find a consistent pattern as to where you are mentally weak. Perhaps you need to work on confidence, or concentration, or self-image. Whatever it is, working on this individual area every day for three to four weeks could change things around.

If you scored 105-117: SUPERIOR MENTAL FITNESS

At this stage, you are, for the most part, usually mentally prepared for races with occasional lapses. If you are in excellent physical shape and can keep up with the best nationally, or in your local age group, you probably finish consistently in the very top—if not first—because you are mentally tough. Slight refinement could give you the edge you've been looking for.

If you scored 118-125: ELITE MENTAL FITNESS

Although you may not be an elite runner, you certainly don't give much away on the mental front. You are probably maximizing much of your potential as a runner, assuming your diet is sound and your physical training is going well. You probably experience many moments of elation from the synchronization of the mind and body. Perhaps this book will help you to "fine-tune" your mental game.

This scoring system has been derived from the years of experience I have had working with many athletes, elite and recreational. A pattern emerges with respect to a runner's attitude toward mental fitness and the level of performance he or she seems to attain. The categories are not an absolute standard; they do indicate, however, where your level of mental fitness may be at this point. As with physical fitness, mental fitness is a skill acquired through daily practice. Therein lies the hope for each and every one of us. You must "work at it" with the same tenacity which you display toward your physical workouts in order to improve. The complete runner trains the body and the mind each day. The ideas and strategies in this book will definitely make a difference in your performance. Your degree of improvement will be directly proportional to the amount of effort you exert being a *total runner*. The competitive edge is now going to those runners who refuse to leave such an important component of the outcome to chance. My prescription for super-performance for runners is: PSYCHLING on a frequent basis. Of course, cycling can't hurt either.

How did it go? Ready to begin a more structured approach to the mental aspects of your performance? Before you do, let me ask you to reflect on the following four basic questions. They will give you a chance to think about some of the more general aspects of your view of yourself with respect to running. I ask these questions of every athlete I work with and discuss their responses as well.

1. HOW WOULD YOU DESCRIBE YOUR OVERALL
    LIFESTYLE?

1	2	3	4	5
Very structured and organized		so-so		Very unstructured and disorganized

It appears that most (80 to 90 percent) of the athletes that I work with who claim to be successful prefer a more structured and organized lifestyle allowing them to get the most out of their training time. They even like it when their training schedule is structured as this gives them indications of how they are progressing. When I work with runners whose lives are in disarray, I can usually predict with fairly good accuracy that their running is erratic as well.

2.   HOW CLOSE DO YOU THINK YOU ARE AT PRESENT TO REACHING YOUR MAXIMUM RUNNING POTENTIAL?

    1   2   3   4   5

Very far away   Halfway there   Very Close

Ideally, I would like to think that "1" is your answer. I believe that one can never really know how close one is to his or her *real* limits. If you think you are close—how do you know? By believing this, what are your chances of going much beyond what you assess your potential to be? This is a tricky one. If you just started to run, perhaps the response should be a "1" or a "2". If you've been running for years and years, you may still be a "2", "3" or "4", depending upon the type of training you've done. If clients answer with a "5", I use that to explore the extent to which they are placing unnecessary barriers upon their abilities. If, indeed, they are "close," there still may be much that can be done which will allow for a significant breakthrough.

3.   WHICH HAS BEEN MOST FREQUENTLY RESPONSIBLE FOR YOUR POORER PERFORMANCES? (Rank these 1 to 4; 1 = most responsible)

    A.   Injuries and illness __1__
    B.   Tactical or judgment error __3__
    C.   Nervous tension __4__
    D.   Inadequate training (physical) __2__

Practically all of the athletes, with a few exceptions, list inadequate training as the least responsible variable; they go into the races well-trained. If they are injured or have been sick, they are likely to delay performance rather than risk further complication. This leaves B and C to share the spotlight as the culprit most likely to interfere with performance. Interestingly enough, if nervous tension persisted in the event, the likelihood for a tactical or judgment error was exponentially increased. When tension was controlled, poor performance due to error was minimized. It appears that once athletes do something about this non-productive tension, performance seems to be consistently better. Asking this question gives my clients a notion about the importance of stress and tension control prior to and during performance. See the chapter on mental race preparation and levels of anxiety.

> 4.   WHICH IS MOST IMPORTANT IN TERMS OF YOUR FEEL-
>   ING GOOD ABOUT A PERFORMANCE?
>   (1 = most important)
>
>   A.   How it compares with my own past performance __1__
>   B.   How it compares with the performance of others in the
>   event __3__
>   C.   How close it comes to a good time (clocktime) __2__

It is interesting to compare elite and recreational runners on this item. Elite, across the board, often respond with B-1, A-2, C-3; recreational enthusiasts score them C-1, B-2, A-3. With respect to the attitudes of the running community and its emphasis on external rewards (trophies, medals, money), it is understandable why B has the highest rating. In other words, most of us seem to feel good if we beat our opponents regardless of how we perform because of the tangible outcome. This is not a "good" or "bad" proposition. I make no value judgments, yet I can say that your *best* efforts will not be realized if you constantly compare the worth of your performance with that of others'. Items B and C require enormous amounts of wasted energy as a result of the anxiety and pressure to "win"; item A can also create pressure, yet unlike B and C, keeping it to yourself can sufficiently reduce that tension. As you will see in the chapter on Attitude Change for Performance, concentrating on competing with yourself will allow you to center all your efforts in a positive direction.

As you embark upon this exciting new journey of integrating the mind with the body, expect to see radical changes as you push back the barriers of what you *thought* were your limits. You are about to use a greater range of your physical and mental resources and actually feel the difference. The inner powers you discover are not new; to paraphrase William James, you already possess those powers—you just habitually fail to use them. I speak about this inner exploration from the perspective of a runner who has experienced the benefits personally, as well as a pscyhologist who understands the theory and applies it accordingly. If benefits are to be had, you must be willing to exercise the mind regularly; as a mind-body runner, you need to train mentally with the same enthusiasm you possess for your physical development. If you do, there is no doubt in my mind that positive changes will take place.

2

The fact that I am able to settle down and physically and mentally relax is one of my greatest strengths. It is something every athlete should seek.

**Rob deCastella
(one of the world's greatest
marathoners—ever)**

Let the Meat Hang on the Bones: Relaxation for Super-Performance

The most widely ignored aspect of training programs in sport happens also to be the most crucial for performance at any level, elite and recreational alike. I am talking about *relaxation*—both mind and body—as a powerful component contributing to excellence in your game of choice. According to Pat Clohessy, coach of the Australian marvel, Rob deCastella, the common denominator of the greatest runners of the past quarter century is their ability to relax. Moses, Snell, Bikila and Mills are some of those who, because of being relaxed, are or were able to easily cope with the pressures of competition.

For Bud Winter, head coach at San Jose State University for 30 years, relaxation was the key to championship performance. As a matter of fact, he has stated that "relaxed running seems so easy it doesn't feel like you are putting out . . . and this is why championship performance in any sport looks smooth and effortless." Who could argue with him when he claimed that relaxation was responsible for much of the success he experienced with his program. Symbols of that success were Olympians Ray Norton, Tommie Smith, John Carlos and Lee Evans, all believers in his policy of letting "the meat hang on the bones." What an image of relaxation. Picture how that feels in the mind. In his classic book, *Relax and Win: Championship Performance in Whatever You Do*, he talks about how his athletes would chant "loose jaw—loose hands" during high pressure moments, and he would ask them to get that "brook-trout look." It was Winter who developed the 90 percent law. When runners try to perform 100 percent, they seem to get anxious and tense. Running at nine-tenths effort is more relaxing and results in faster speed.

New Zealand runners have also been exposed to the concept of relaxation under the positive influence of the great Arthur Lydiard. His coaching emphasizes relaxation, particularly during the base building season when his runners would take easy jaunts over hill and dale, exploring the beautiful countryside near Auckland. Running with one of his students, world master marathon champion, John Robinson, during his 1980 summer stay in Boulder, Colorado, I began to understand the importance of running relaxed. John and I would often roam the foothills cutting trails and simply enjoy the beauty of the Rockies at a very relaxing, easy pace.

Regardless of the event, whether it's a sprint, the long jump, the shot put, the high jump, the discus, the mile, or all the distance events, an ability to relax seems to be a necessary prerequisite to success. My working with the athletes at the U.S. Olympic Training Center has reinforced this belief. Without exception, elite marathoners propose that the secret to smoother, faster running is to concentrate on becoming more relaxed, rather than efforting more power. Efforting causes muscular tightness and a decrease in the synchronicity between the hamstrings and the quadriceps. The hamstrings need to be relaxed as the quads are turned on in order to run efficiently. Relaxation facilitates this process. This can be crucial in the last stages of a marathon, when the body begins to tighten and the pressure mounts; those that stay cool, loose and relaxed prevail. Alberto Salazar attributes his strength in the final moments of his marathon victories to his ability to remain calm . . . relaxed. His picture, plastered on every running magazine cover after his stellar world class performance in New York, was an incredible caricature of the "brook-trout look," so often referred to by Coach Winter. Imitating the look on his face could help you to become more relaxed as well.

RELAXATION DEFINED

Relaxation is a state of physical and mental stillness, or quiet, characterized by the absence of tension and anxiety. During this state, the heart rate decreases, as does the amount of oxygen consumed. Breathing becomes consistently regular and the muscles "let go" as tensions dissipate. Mentally, the brain wave pattern slows considerably to what is called an *alpha state,* a very healthful state of consciousness that increases one's concentration away from non-productive self-criticism toward a more productive anxiety-free focus—a frame of mind more conducive to successful performance. Such a mind set enables one to focus entirely on the task at hand, by tuning out internal and external distraction. Relaxation is a valuable tool to be used before, during and after a selected performance. The next section will elaborate upon this.

BENEFITS OF RELAXATION

The positive effects of calming the body are innumerable. Athletes, in particular, increase the probabilty of a good performance exponentially with the regular practice of relaxation. The following are some of the more powerful benefits for runners:

1. Muscles become more fluid. It helps distance runners to keep their antagonistic (unused) muscles relaxed and, therefore, run with as few muscles as possible. As a result, coordination and endurance improve.

2. Lowers stress. Relaxation creates an optimal level of arousal and keeps in check inappropriate and useless stress. As a result, less energy is burned. Also, you become less prone to injury and illness.

3. Clears the mind. The alpha state inhibits the "chatter" of the mind which tends to improve concentration. With improved concentration, success probability increases followed by a rise in confidence. Increased confidence improves self-image and we perform according to our self-image 90 percent of the time. Therefore, success is more likely to occur.

4. Creates vivid images. When the mind is clear and relaxed, it allows one to visualize beyond just "seeing"; all the senses can be used to full benefit during this state: "hear" the crowds, "feel" the equipment, "taste" the ERG (electrolyte replacement drink), "smell" the grass or the auditorium.

5. Lowers blood lactate. Although it's unclear exactly how this happens, research shows that with relaxation, blood lactate (the accumulation of which inhibits performance) decreases.

6. Reduces fatigue. Anxiety causes the muscles to be in a constant state of contraction which then inhibits the flow of blood to those

muscles. Physiological fatigue is the result of decreased blood flow to these regions and relaxation can reverse this process.

7. Regenerates the body and mind. Deep relaxation reduces excessive pressure and you begin to recapture the pleasure of running.

8. Expands reality. Relaxation provides an opportunity to suspend normal expectations about perceived reality and try new imagined results that go beyond your established belief system. You begin to "experience" a reality that exceeds self-imposed limitations.

TIME TO RELAX

The most frequently asked questions with regard to relaxation are: when do I do it; for how long; and, how often? My general response is that "more is definitely better." The only time I recommend *not* doing it is within one hour after a big meal. The body needs to concentrate on digestion and there is also a greater risk of falling asleep during the exercise if preceded by a big meal.

My advice for maximal benefits is to "work out" mentally once a day for ten to fifteen minutes; for those of you with a busy schedule, consider the time prior to rising in the morning or just before going to bed at night. If you have a tendency to fall back to sleep in the morning, reset the alarm clock before you relax. Many of my clients prefer a 15-minute session during their lunch hour, prior to eating. My personal choice is to take a number of five-minute "time-outs" throughout the day, prior to an activity such as teaching my classes, counseling a client or running a workout. Whatever you choose, the key is *consistency*. Incorporate it into your day along with other automatic behaviors—eating, running, working . . . relaxing. The more you practice, the easier it becomes and the quicker you can achieve a state of complete calm. In fifteen seconds, I can be functioning in an alpha state of relaxation. In all fairness to yourself and the process, give the chosen relaxation technique 21 days; I will predict, with 95 percent certainty, that positive changes will occur if you do.

APPLICATION OF RELAXATION

Calming the mind and body is an excellent way to achieve overall health and well-being on a day-to-day basis. More specifically, relaxation techniques can be applied to improving training runs and racing performance, as well as facilitating post-event emotional and physical recovery. I suggest using relaxation techniques in conjunction with the following situations:

1. Prior to visualization. Many athletes visualize, yet overlook the importance of preceding it with relaxation. Calming the body and reaching an alpha state allows the mind to visualize with *all* senses, thereby creating images that are extremely powerful. Concentration on these images is enhanced, increasing the probability of that scenario being repeated in reality.

2. Prior to the competition. All competition carries with it a heightened level of arousal that could be counter-productive to performance. Use relaxation to regulate that stress to an optimum level (see chapter on Competitive Psychling). The more difficult the task, the less experienced you are or the more important the event, the closer to the commencement of the event should you do your relaxation.

3. Prior to a workout. Quite often, the body seems lethargic before your training run, particularly if the day has been stressful. Using relaxation can regenerate that lost energy by relaxing the muscles and increasing the blood flow. Calming can also decrease blood lactate levels which impede movement.

4. Post-workout or competition. After strenuous physical exertion, the body becomes physically unbalanced and tense, setting the stage for possible trauma. Relaxation restores equilibrium to the body and reduces the risk of injury. Recovery processes will speed up.

5. During a workout or competition. Fatigue, tired and tightened sore muscles, distraction and tactical errors are the result of, or cause, anxiety. Regardless of the tension's etiology, such hindrances to performance can best be resolved by relaxing the body, the mind or a combination of both. How you do this will depend on the nature of the event and its duration. For example, a sprinter hasn't the time to relax the mind during a 100-meter dash; however, for a marathoner, this is quite possible. The method you choose will be specifically geared to your event.

6. Developing new abilities. Whether you are working on improving form, understanding a new concept or practicing a different skill, the apprentice state will be greatly enhanced through

relaxation. Calming the mind and body prior to the practice session will enable you to assimilate the new task more effectively and swiftly.

"HOW-TO" TECHNIQUES FOR RELAXATION

There is absolutely no one *right* way to relax. It is an individual process; whatever works for you is the *right* way. I discovered an interesting "new" method to induce relaxation recently when I showed up for an important race without my racing flats (I didn't follow my own advice in the chapter on " . . . your mental best on race day"). The dilapidated shoes I wore to the 10-kilometer event would not do it. My running buddy suggested I wear his training shoes, quite a bit heavier and a half-size too big. I had no choice as I already paid the entry fee and was primed for a run. With no expectations other than to run a good workout, the pressure was off. I glided through the effort, running the race of my life, and recorded a personal best in the process. I learned quite a bit that day.

Perhaps you have discovered a unique method that works best for you. I refuse to suggest that the following strategies should replace what works; they may, however, offer some interesting options and variations to your program. If you need something new, then I'm sure one of these, or a combination of a few, will help you to achieve a state of quiet relaxation. Some techniques will actually be demonstrated; others will be explained and you will be referred to another source for further details.

1. DEEP COUNTDOWN BREATHING: This is one of my favorites. Most athletes seem to use this method because it's easy to learn, it gets the participant relaxed quickly and deeply and results are easily noticeable. When perfected it can produce a calming stillness in 15 seconds, regardless of whether you are lying, sitting or standing. Logistically, it is one of the most practical methods. When learning it, I suggest you practice in a comfortable prone position, with eyes closed, in a cozy place, devoid of noise and distraction. If you think you'll fall asleep, try sitting up—this will prevent or delay "dozing off." Follow these steps:

    ● Place your hands on your abdomen, right below the navel. Fingertips of each hand should touch one another.

- Breathe through the nostrils; mouth breathing is not as relaxing.

- Inhale *very slowly;* as you do, push the abdomen out as though it were a balloon expanding. Your fingers should separate.

- As the abdomen expands, your diaphragm will move downward, allowing fresh air to enter the bottom of the lungs.

- As the breath continues, expand the chest. More air will enter, filling the middle part of the lungs.

- Next, raise your shoulders and collarbones. This should fill the upper part of the lungs completely.

- The entire respiratory system has been employed. *Hold breath for three to five seconds.*

- After holding breath, begin *slowly* to exhale through the nostrils. As you do, draw in the abdomen. This will lift the diaphragm and the lungs will empty. It is important to exhale properly.

- Remember to exhale very slowly. If comfortable, hold it a few seconds before beginning the inhalation process again.

Repeat this process for five breaths (or more if needed) and, as you do, count down 5-4-3-2-1, saying one number as you exhale each time, in descending order. As you approach number 1, "feel" yourself get deeper and deeper into a relaxed state. While in this state, let your mind *visualize* (see Chapter 3 for techniques on mental imagery) and rehearse. After the first few tries, you can drop your hands away from your abdomen; they are only there to help you experience your stomach pushing out. Also, you need to determine the number of breaths you need to feel relaxed. With practice, you'll be in a deep, relaxed state in three breaths. Remember to breathe deeply, but *not* forcefully, as that may defeat the purpose of relaxing as well as causing you to hyperventilate. If you begin to experience a slight dizzy feeling during the initial practice sessions, that's normal; ease up a bit on the deepness of the breath. Results will occur from regular, daily, five-minute sessions; again, more is better.

USES: This technique is best used on a daily basis, prior to a task or when a task has been completed. Other than in isolated instances, it's diffiuclt to employ during most running events.

It's extremely useful for mental imagery rehearsal, injury healing, pre-event jitters and anxiety, concentration, fears and overall mind-body wellness.

2. PROGRESSIVE MUSCLE RELAXATION: The following is a variation of the method discovered in the 1920s by a Chicago physician, Dr. Edmund Jacobson. While working with hyper-tense patients, he found that if you flexed a muscle to tension, held that tension for a few seconds, then released it, the muscle became more relaxed. There seems to be a feedback mechanism in the muscle tissue that signals it to overreact in the opposite direction. Additionally, the patients also learned what tension actually felt like; thus, they could identify those times when a muscle was tight and respond appropriately.

This phase of relaxation is important to the relief of tenseness in the muscles which hinders coordination and performance. Following three or four sessions, you may be able to attain complete muscle relaxation within five to seven minutes. Remember to preface this exercise with a few minutes of abdominal breathing.

- Be sure to wear clothing that is not binding; lie on something comfortable; keep arms a few inches from the body; eyes closed.

- Relax with breathing; let your weight sink downward; do not exert any effort in trying to relax; just be loose.

- *Slowly* stiffen the muscles in both arms. Don't move arms or clench fists.

- Hold for 10 seconds at a slight degree of stiffness; stiffen a little more and hold for 10 seconds or so.

- Observe how your arms feel during that 10 seconds. Are they mildly sore or tender? Consciously recognizing these signs of contracted muscles is the first step in learning deep muscle relaxation.

- Allow your arms to relax gradually; notice how the stiffness becomes less intense. Rest in the relaxed state for a minute or two.

- Repeat the entire procedure again; tighten and hold in progressive states; hold the last stages each time for half a minute, then relax gradually.

- After you have mastered the arms, try the exercise with the legs, abdomen, chest and facial muscles. Use the same progressive manner.

After about four sessions, you should be able to omit the stage of tensing that precedes the relaxation of the muscles as its purpose is simply to familiarize you with what it's like to feel tense. Once familiar, you will be able to go directly to the area where tension is being experienced and relax that particular muscle group by "letting go" and visualizing it melting away like a snowball under intense heat.

USES: This technique can be used just prior to any event quite successfully. Also, some runners have tried relaxing the shoulder, neck and face areas during a race using the "tensing-let go" procedure. Used in conjunction with the breathing, you can create an even deeper state of relaxation; expecially prior to visualization.

3. FACE MASK RELAXATION: It is commonly known that the facial muscles, to a great extent, control the tension in the rest of the body. Simply relax the face and you will create a looseness all over. As an experiment, frown and clench your jaw and see how tense you become. The jaw, neck, eyes and forehead are those most often responsible for facial tightness.

To help alleviate this tension, create in your mind a soft, smooth rubber mask. Gently "pull" it over your head and, as it slides over the face, it irons out the wrinkles and effortlessly supports your jaw. It allows you to get those "soft eyes" where they slightly droop and become half-closed. This face mask enables to you "let go" because it will hold everything together for you.

USES: This method is especially useful while on the run. Observe others running and notice how serious they look. Their faces are tight and clinched. The mask method will facilitate Bud Winter's "brook-trout look." Non-productive "efforting" starts and stops with the face.

4. CUE WORD RELAXATION: This is not a specific relaxation technique, as such, but when paired with other exercises, the cue word becomes a stimulus for the relaxed state. For example, every time you exhale in technique number one, or "let go" of the tension in number two, say the word "calm," or "r-e-l-a-x,"

or "o-n-e." By so doing, you are strengthening the association between that cue word and the relaxed state.

With enough practice, it can be used in competition to become instantly calm, much like a computer tapping its stored bits of information. As you say your cue word, feel the peaceful stillness spread throughout your body. You now have a reference point for relaxation.

5. TRANSCENDENTAL MEDITATION (TM): This is a simple method originating in ancient India and adapted for the Western world by Maharishi Yogi. Like the cue word, it involves the use of a *mantra* (man = to think; tra = to liberate), a sound or meaningless word individually assigned to the participant; its use reduces tension and quiets the mind. Advocates claim that TM has a powerful influence on the mind and facilitates performance as well as confidence. You learn the technique by registering

and paying for a course at one of the many TM centers around the country. There are many variations and imitations of TM that some people have found just as helpful and less expensive. All create a state of relaxation.

6. BIOFEEDBACK: There are many times when it is difficult to detect when and where tension arises. We live with it constantly and, as a result, become oblivious to its presence. Being unaware, however, does not prevent it from interfering with performance. Biofeedback is the use of machinery to create an awareness of your present biological state: muscle tension, brain wave activity, blood pressure and heart rate. It detects those bodily components which are not relaxed and increases awareness of what it feels like to have inner calm and silence. It is best used as a supplement to other relaxation techniques. Once you improve the ability to locate the tension, the machine should no longer be needed; once identified, you then need relaxation exercises to facilitate the "letting go" process. Although the industry is developing inexpensive monitoring equipment, biofeedback still requires the outlay of money, and the need to locate a machine. However, if you live near a big university or college, I suggest that you visit the Psychology Department and ask if they have any instruments you can use. Oftentimes, they conduct research studies and would be more than happy to give you the feedback data in return for your participation in their program. For information regarding bio-feedback practitioners in your area, write: Biofeedback Society of America, 4301 Owen Street, Wheatridge, Colorado 80030.

7. SELF-HYPNOSIS: I have used self-hypnosis with athletes and report wonderful results. Many of these athletes are finding that this technique is responsible for major breakthroughs in their sport. It can be used to relax, to make positive life changes, to increase concentration exponentially, reduce fatigue and improve performance. It is fast and easy to learn. It can be self-taught or learned from someone trained in the technique. Good bookstores carry a wide selection of reading in this area. For starters, try Freda Morris: *Self-Hypnosis in Two Days* (1974).

8. FLOTATION TANK THERAPY: Athletes are discovering powerful positive effects on performance as a result of floating weightlessly in a tank containing water 10 inches deep in which 800 pounds or more of Epsom salts have been dissolved in the

water. The solution is so dense that you bob like a whiffle ball on the ocean. Those who have used this technique claim that, for the first time in their lives, they begin to experience real relaxation. They say the effects of one float can last for up to three weeks, although that is unusual. Researchers of flotation say that individuals actually experience a lower adrenal activation rate. If this is so, the implications for competitive athletic pressure are enormous; perhaps no more choking.

Other claims, although not substantially researched, show the flotation system capable of speeding up recovery from injury, decreasing or eliminating pain and, most impressively, asserting that the ability to visualize while floating is exponentially more powerful than it is in a hypnotic state alone. It could very well be the new "breakthrough" technique for optimal performance. More research needs to be carried out; I suggest you give it a try and decide what it does for you personally.

9. ZEN AND YOGA: These represent an Eastern form of meditation and relaxation. They are best practiced in a quiet environment where distraction is minimal. Research has shown that the monks and yogis are capable of decreasing heart rate, metabolism and oxygen consumption by as much as 20 percent. This has implications for improved performance as well as deep relaxation.

10. MISCELLANEOUS: Grouping these together in last place is not a commentary on their importance or effectivess to relaxation; I have listed them as such because their effect on calming the body needs no explanation. We just need to remind ourselves about these alternatives—try them in combination or individually:

Hot tub, music, candlelight, sauna, steam room, and, of course, *running,* particularly alone.

RUNNING RELAXED

While the foregoing techniques will contribute to greater relaxation for better performance, don't overlook the enormous effect of *running style* on the conservation of energy and facilitation of relaxation.

Attention to the following principles will help you to run more smoothly, efficiently and calmly:

a. Get that "brook-trout look"; slacken the jaw. This will relax much of the entire body.

b. Keep upper body perpendicular to the surface. Pull shoulders back slightly and push the buttocks forward.

c. Keep hands softly closed as if you were holding on to delicate paper cylinders.

d. Stride smoothly. Try to avoid over- and under-striding as these waste incredible amounts of energy.

e. Relax the shoulders and carry arms low. Shoulders should remain loose yet stable. Elbows can be firm but not locked. The tip of your thumb ought to brush by your waist at the point where the top of a pocket would be.

f. Move faster by focusing on r-e-l-a-x-a-t-i-o-n rather than on applying *power*.

In the words of Fred Rohe from his book, *The Zen of Running*, "Feel the flow of the dance and know you are not running for some future reward—for the reward is now!"

This chapter has prepared you for the remainder of the book. The strategies and techniques discussed are the basis of any sound program for mental preparation and super-performance. With consistent practice and persistence, you will begin to experience positive results. Like physical training, the mind needs time to develop. You should see changes in your running after 21 days of daily practice; maybe even sooner.

I caution you that it is difficult to develop the habit of relaxation, particularly since the payoff, at first, may be minimal. Remember how it was when you first started to run? After six months, you were probably hooked. With these exercises, you will never experience their powerful effects unless you decide to not excuse yourself from doing them. If your dream is to improve performance to the point where your optimal potential is realized, you are on the right track. Without the proper use of the mind, the dream will fade; with it, your dream will become a reality. Stick with your effort—it requires patience and persistence, and a minimum amount of time. Before you actually begin the journey toward super-performance, I recommend that you read at least the first five chapters of this book; this will also enhance your probability of a successful program.

3

Our images are self-fulfilling prophecies. What we envision is what we get.

**Adelaide Bry
(author of *Visualization:
Directing the Movies of
Your Mind*)**

Mind Movies:
Creating Success
Through Visualization

Many hundreds of years ago in ancient China, a famous, accomplished concert pianist was incarcerated by the opposing faction for his participation in a regional uprising. After eight years of solitary confinement, he became a free man. Four weeks into his "new" life, he put on a performance that was judged by his peers to have gone beyond anything he had ever done. Amazed by this, they asked how this could be possible having been in an empty cell for so long. He stated that he diligently rehearsed for this concert for hours each day. But there was no piano, they said. His reply was that although they took the instrument, they left the mind: he "felt" the keys; "saw" his hands sliding across them; "heard" the intricate melodies; and "smelled" the perspiration on his body after an arduous "recital." Amazing? Not really!

The use of *visualization* techniques for improved performance is not new as evidenced by this story. The disciplines of yoga and meditation from ancient India, eastern martial arts and hypnosis are other examples from the past where the mind's pictures were an integral aspect of one's performance. Today, visualization has found its way into the sports arena where sophisticated athletes, refusing to leave the outcome of performance to chance, train the mind and body in synchronous fashion.

VISUALIZATION: WHAT IT IS AND IS NOT

Most of us have "seen," at one time or another, the outcome of an event before it actually occurred. Thoughts about how an event will unfold are not, however, necessarily the process of visualization. More often than not, such patterns are *visual thinking processes* that take place consciously or unconsciously calling upon one sense modality—sight. Sometimes the thoughts are pleasant and productive; often, they represent catastrophic expectations arising from one's fear of failure. Visualization, on the other hand, is the conscious use of the imagination during a deep state of relaxation to enhance performance through the use of all sense modalities. Visualizing a run means you can "see," "hear" and "feel" yourself moving; you may even "taste" the water on the run and "smell" the perspiration as a result of hard work. This is all made possible because the relaxed state stops the "chatter" in the mind and allows you to focus sharply on the experience. Surely you have had a dream that seemed so real that upon awakening, it was a welcome relief not to be falling. Such is the nature of visualization in the alpha state of relaxation. Quite simply, the images are so alive that your central nervous system recognizes little qualitative differences between a real or imagined event; your body responds to each in the same way. Close your eyes and concentrate on a juicy lemon wedge; imagine biting into it. Notice how your mouth begins to fill with saliva. If an athlete can picture each movement of the event correctly beforehand, the greater the chances of those movements being repeated during the actual event.

Visualization is not magic or hocus-pocus. It is a learned skill and, when practiced regularly, it can change your life. Although the greatest of minds struggle to comprehend the workings of the mind, there are scientific explanations that describe the process of visualization (I will come to that) and why it is so effective. In actuality, you put it to work each day and see the results; it is called imagination and we use it rather unconsciously. For example, many people have negative pictures about life; they imagine catastrophe, limits, problems and doom. And that's what they get. If things do go well, it's because they had positive images, yet it happened by chance—as luck would have it. Visualization is the process of controlling those images each day so as to increase the chances of positive occurrences. Of course, no amount of visualization will give you the impossible; it will simply help you not to lose what you deserve as a result of negative mind programming. Still skeptical? Good—read on!

The fact that visualization works is no secret to Olympic Biathlete, Lyle Nelson. His is a demanding sport which combines cross-country skiing and rifle shooting. In a recent phone conversation with Lyle, he related to me his image of being like the Rock of Gibraltar just prior to the shooting section of his event to acquire a calm steadiness. He attributes his success in this event to his visualization skills. Coach Peter Karns of the U.S. Biathalon Team credits visualization with the team's fantastic improvement at the 1976 Winter Olympics.

In a recent television interview, champion tennis star, Chris Evert-Lloyd, stated that she practices visualization prior to competition. For the first time in 14 matches, she had the mental attitude that she could beat her nemesis, Martina Navratilova, thanks to visualization. The outcome was an Evert-Lloyd triumph.

Jack Nicklaus, in his book, *Golf My Way*, talks about having very sharp, distinct images in his head prior to each shot.

Physiologist Dave Martin, who works with high jumper Dwight Stones, tells me that Dwight rehearses each step of the jump two or three times before he takes off. Anyone watching the 1984 Olympics could see his head nodding each precise move, including the leap itself.

The list of elite athletes in the running world using visualization to bring about their best could fill pages of this book: Lee Evans, Steve Scott, Dick Beardsley, Herb Lindsay, Joan Benoit, Julie Brown and Tony Sandoval have all been known to take advantage of "the mind's eye." While working together at the U.S. Olympic Training Center in Colorado Springs, Sandoval related to me how he visualized the entire 1980 Olympic Marathon trials in advance, "hearing" splits, "feeling" surges and other facets of the race in explicit detail. As we all know, he won the gold medal on that day.

The wonderful thing about visualization is, you don't have to be an elite or professional athlete to benefit. You will learn the essential ingredients of this technique in this chapter and,with some practice, it will be yours. As you exercise the mind, you will make it stronger; the more you experience success in your pictures, the more energy you will create that will enable success to be experienced.

HOW IS THIS ALL POSSIBLE?

As a young boy enthused about being a great basketball player (it ceased to be a dream because realistically, I wasn't tall enough), I would watch on television the "moves" of Bob Cousy (star of the

Boston Celtics), then go to the schoolyard and imitate his style. I played my best ball on those days. Watching the experts perform seems to improve the quality of your game because the body understands and responds to vivid, detailed images. Recreational golf and tennis players frequently report improved performances following the Crosby Pro-Am Golf Tourney, or the U.S. Open Tennis matches on television; the pros model the perfect images for excellence in sport. Physiologically, it has been shown that images create measurable amounts of contraction in those muscles used for specific tasks. For example, I recently experienced a group of runners hooked up to an electromyograph machine (EMG, measures muscle movement). Lying on tables, they were asked to imagine running up a difficult hill. Those muscles required to propel the body on such terrain became activated and were recorded on the EMG equipment, even thought the athletes were lying still. If you would like to experience the effect of images on muscle response in reverse, try this exercise. While lying down, legs uncrossed and out straight, go to a deep level of relaxation using the deep breathing method from Chapter 2. When totally relaxed, imagine the lower parts of your legs becoming covered with concrete. "See" it being poured; "feel" the coolness and texture. As it dries, notice how it solidifies and encases your legs. Take another deep breath (number six) and, as you exhale, gently try to lift your feet. Don't strain. Notice the heaviness of the concrete and how difficult it is to budge that part of your body. Anatomists have shown that images have a powerful impact on every cell in our bodies. It is important to understand this phenomenon as a runner. The muscle groups involved in your forward motion are activated totally by images. Your visualization enables messages to be sent, on a subliminal level, through your nervous system, to those muscles. Aside from its effect on muscles, research is now showing that visualization can actually change blood pressure, heart rate, body temperature and other functions of the body once thought to be involuntary physiological processes.

Another reason why visualization works, aside from this physiological explanation, is the self-fulfilling prophecy. Verbally repeat and imagine something often enough and it will come to pass. Athletes who often repeat an image during visualization exercises of what they would want to happen during a performance, actually begin to expect that outcome to occur. This expectation causes the athlete to behave in ways that enhance the possibility of the desired outcome becoming a reality. If you "see" yourself as a winner, you will act that way 90 percent of the time and thereby dramatically increase the chances of being that winner. (See chapter on Self-Image.) The body responds to the language of images (the senses). Prophesize a desire by using the senses—feel, hear, smell, taste and see— and the body will fulfill that wish. Expect satisfaction, happiness and success, and you will create an environment of people, situations and occurrences which will fulfill those expectations.

On a more basic plane, visualization works because it resembles a dress rehearsal. It is a form of practice which increases familiarity with the task. As you will see in the chapter on mental race preparation, you can, in the mind, "work out the kinks" before they actually happen; since the central nervous system does not distinguish between a real or imagined event, the mind will interpret an imagined tactical race error as if it were real. Your positive response to that error during visualization will increase the possibility of your responding favorably should such an error happen to occur in reality.

ESSENTIAL INGREDIENTS FOR VISUALIZATION

Like any skills to be learned, visualization has a number of essential components which, if included in the process, increase its effectiveness. The following must be present if you wish to maximize the benefits of visualization:

- BELIEF IN THE OUTCOME. To have a lackadaisical attitude toward the outcome tells your mind that you really don't care and what you are doing is not important. The stronger your belief, the stronger impression on the brain you will make. Believe and you'll receive.

- DESIRE THE OUTCOME. You only attempt to accomplish that which you desire. The obvious example is your desire to live; you program yourself to survive. With visualization, you must have a true desire to have that which you ask for. It is the sense of a clear, strong purpose and commitment. (See Chapter 4 on Commitment.)

- EXPECT THE OUTCOME. You must assume that the outcome is not only very possible, but that it will occur as conceived. It is the feeling you have when you turn on the faucet—you expect water to flow and it usually does.

- PRECEDE WITH RELAXATION. As you discovered in Chapter 2 on Relaxation, most athletes omit this stage in the visualization process. Such a calm state of mind is essential to clear, vivid, powerful imagery. You need to silence the "chatter" of the mind if the body is to get the correct message.

- USE ALL SENSES. The more senses you can call into play, the stronger the imagery and the greater the chances for a successful outcome. You will notice that you identify with certain senses and find others more difficult to relate to. That's natural. Use those that are your strongest and, in time, the others will come as you train the mind to think in this way. Try to "smell" the rubbing cream, "feel" your body glide over the course, "taste" the post-race refreshments, "see" the sky and "hear" the crowd. Let your imagination run wild.

- BE SPECIFIC. Your images will have a more powerful effect if they are specific to every detail of the game plan. When you rehearse a finishing time, be precise: 2:41:27—right to the second. Be sure to visualize exactly what you want and nothing else. You not only want to run a marathon in a precise time, but you want to feel healthy and physically whole after the event. "See" that happen.

- VISUALIZE THE POSITIVE. When you imagine an outcome or a process, be sure to state it positively. For example, avoid saying "I am not tired," or "I am not injured." Instead, state that "I have lots of energy" and "I am healthy and strong." Stating the negative may confuse the mind and it could pick up on the words 'tired' and 'injured.'

- VISUALIZE VIA IMAGERY OR REHEARSAL. Depending upon your goal, you may choose to "see" or "feel" youself performing. To change a bad habit or correct a mistake, "see" yourself running on a big screen as if watching a movie. This process, called imagery, works well for those of you who are visually oriented. Some people are more kinesthetic and prefer to "feel" themselves perform from the inside looking out. Either way is legitimate; the "feel" approach happens to be more powerful because sport is primarily physical in nature. This approach is called rehearsal. Try both methods and see how you respond.

- BE PATIENT AND CONSISTENT. Changes take time. Give yourself about three weeks before you see the benefits. They could happen sooner. Also, it is better to visualize five minutes a day for one week rather than 35 minutes once in seven days. The key is consistency. If you miss a day or two, it doesn't matter that much. Just begin again. As you start to see results and feel good, you will become addicted and use it more often.

- FOCUS ON THE PROCESS. When visualizing, "see" your goals then let them be. Accomplish this by focusing on the process that will lead you to those goals. You must experience the feeling involved before, during and after the event, be it a race or a workout. Feeling good throughout will increase the chances of a great performance and the goals will come as a result.

WHEN TO UTILIZE THE TECHNIQUE

Since most of our behavior and actions follow our images, the technique of visualization is applicable to almost all life's experiences; I have trained a broad spectrum of people in the utilization of these concepts—from corporate workers to athletes to ballet dancers and musicians—all of whom have had at least one goal in common: optimal performance. Generally, the time to use visualization is whenever you need to gain greater control over a situation or maximize the outcome so that the best happens. Try applying it to your workouts, to the race itself, before, during and after. The following list is a more specific account of when to employ this method. Each example can also be viewed as a benefit of the process of visualization.

Uses and Benefits

1. To intensify relaxation by creating a peaceful, pastoral scene.
2. To optimize the chances of a good workout, prior to its occurrence.
3. To optimize the chances of a good race, prior to its occurrence.
4. To help cope with fatigue.
5. To help overcome obstacles during a performance. "Feel" a balloon lifting you up a hill; "see" yourself as a wedge cutting through the wind.

6. To help create a realistic, workable self-image for optimal per-
    formance.

7. To reduce the fear of failure.

8. To facilitate the process of goal setting

9. To help prevent and treat injuries.

10. To simulate the unknown in a race and practice responding in a
    desirable fashion.

11. To help cope with post-race feelings of frustration and disap-
    pointment.

12. To create an image of how you wish to run; modeling an expert.

13. To help increase levels of concentration by focusing on one
    image.

14. To recapture that "feeling" of an ideal past performance to
    increase confidence.

15. To pretend that you're an animal running smoothly and
    effortlessly.

16. To imprint in your memory an excellent performance
    immediately following it.

17. To review tactical errors made in a race and rerun the event in
    your mind with the changes you would like to make for future
    races.

18. To change beliefs and, as a result, push back the boundaries of
    your limits.

19. To heighten level of enjoyment.

20. To improve quality of learning new skills.

21. To help restore energy level.

22. To help raise level of motivation.

23. To reduce level of anxiety

24. To self-regulate level of arousal for optimal competitive tension.

25. To assist in the regulation of blood pressure and heart-pulse rate.

Many of these uses and benefits of visualization are discussed
and explained in chapters throughout this book. This list is far from
being exhaustive, yet it should get you started in the right direction.
Be creative and expand upon these to meet your specific needs.
Remember that anything can be visualized; you are always imagining

events in life. The key to creating a desirable outcome is to consciously control your thoughts using the section in this chapter on essential ingredients for successful visualization.

VISUALIZATION EXERCISES FOR RUNNERS

Now that you have a clearer idea of how and when to visualize, it's time to practice the skill and to experience how it feels. If this is your first try at the process, it is probably best to start with basic, simple images and then advance to the more complex. No matter how good your skills are, there is always room for improvement.

The following exercises will give you an indication of how well you can image sport-related pictures. The questions are adapted from Gordon's test of visual imagery control in *Mental Imagery* by A. Richardson. Get into a relaxed position in a quiet environment, read each question, then close your eyes and visualize what was just read. Check "yes," "no," or "unsure" to indicate your visualization capability.

		Yes	No	Unsure
1.	Can you see yourself in your warmups?			
2.	Can you see it in color?			
3.	Can you see yourself stretching?			
4.	Can you see yourself running along the road?			
5.	Can you see yourself running up a steep hill?			
6.	Can you see yourself running as the race starts?			
7.	Can you see yourself relaxed in a tense situation?			
8.	Can you see yourself milling around after the race?			

Continue your visualization with the following exercise which will test your ability to use all senses; concentrate on creating visual images:

- SIGHT: see a tree as it sways in the wind
             see a child learning to ride a bike
             see yourself standing just prior to the start of a race

- SOUND: hear the sound of your feet hitting the road as you race
             hear the sound of your favorite piece of music
             hear the clapping of hands from the crowd at
                 the finish line

- TOUCH: feel the bottom of your running shoes
             feel the water of a warm bath or shower
             feel yourself pick up sand and have it fall through
                 your fingers

- TASTE: taste orange wedges after a race
             taste a slice of cherry cheese cake
             taste a glass of water

- SMELL: smell the inside of your running shoes
             smell the grass that has just been mowed
             smell burning leaves

Notice which senses are most developed and which need the most work. In time, your imagination will become quite sophisticated with practice. The more senses you use, the more beneficial the experience will be for performance.

In her book, *Creative Visualization,* Shakti Gawain suggests that when you start using mental imagery, the first thing you should do is to create, in your mind, a place of peace. This sanctuary is your ideal place of inner calm and tranquility. Once there, you can use visualization as you wish. It becomes a place to return to just by closing your eyes and relaxing. It will give you the safety and security you need during times of deep thought. The exercise is enjoyable and powerful:

- Close your eyes. Relax using your personal method. In a comfortable position, imagine yourself in some beautiful, natural environment; let it be any place that appeals to you—perhaps you have
  actually been there before or maybe you are creating it for the first
  time. Is it a meadow, or a mountain home in a beautiful forest, or

near the ocean on a beach? It should feel comfortable and peaceful to you. Notice all details, sounds, smells and feelings of the environment. Perhaps you would like to have a home there. What would it look like? Arrange the inside in any way you wish. Is there a big deck? If so, see yourself looking over the terrain. You are in control of this script, so create the scene exactly as you would want it. As you become more familiar with it, your comfort level will increase. Return often whenever the need to be alone and think arises. From this place of peace, you can do all your visual programming. You may even want to go for a run on the beach or trails while "vacationing" in this sanctuary. Allow changes to occur in this environment as the need dictates. Be creative—it's your private place. If you could benefit from a hot tub, install one and "feel" yourself relaxing in the intense heat.

One excellent way to use this place of peace is to recapture the feeling of past success in order to build confidence prior to compe-

tition. This readying technique, called *revivification*, is the process of going back to those moments when you felt terrific—ready to run, a little nervous perhaps, but knowing that all systems are go. It was a time when your performance was remarkable. What did that feel like? What were your thoughts? Try to recreate the scene in detail— the weather, the crowd, the exhilaration, the effortless glide, feeling like you could run forever. Recapturing this feeling in your place of peace will enable the body to be in a state of peaceful readiness. If you practice this visual exercise often, you will be able to recreate that feeling at crucial moments before and during the competition. Of all the techniques talked about in this book, this is probably the single most important in terms of super-performance; your body will respond to these images as if they were actually happening in the present. Your performance should follow accordingly.

As you become more proficient with the skill of visualization, you may wish to try a procedure called: *detachment training*. This is the process of becoming relaxed and trying to focus with actual irritating noises and distractions in the background. Start by blasting the stereo and trying to go to an alpha state. When you get good at that, add some people to the room and tell them what you're doing. The purpose of such training is to simulate "game time" with all its concomitant frenzy. What I find helpful is to imagine a mental wall (plexiglass shield) surrounding my body; noise and distractions bounce off the shield like a bullet-proof vest. Nothing can penetrate other than necessary information announcing an emergency situation. I try not to use effort keeping the background out; I simply concentrate on what I deem important.

There are some other interesting exercises that I recommend to you when on leisurely training runs. These "mind games" are very enjoyable and results are usually immediate. When you become accomplished with them, use those you enjoy most during your next competition.

- Imagine youself floating in front of the lead pack at the New York City Marathon
- As you run up a tough hill, visualize being suspended by helium balloons or being gently guided and pushed by a giant hand on the small of your back

- Let your running partner get in front of you if he or she seems to have more energy. Imagine a rainbow connecting your heads together and begin to feel your partner's energy flow through the rainbow into your body
- As you run into the wind, imagine you are shaped like a wedge and cut through the breeze effortlessly
- Imagine yourself to be an animal with grace, style and strength
- As you descend off a high hill, look out into the distance and feel like a giant bird, floating to your destination
- Imagine your body to be a well-greased, oiled and highly tuned machine, with all parts moving in synchronicity
- During a track workout, see yourself floating by the cheering crowds. They all came to see you set a new world record on the mile
- Create your own; there are limitless possibilities

Perhaps one of the more powerful exercises with regard to visualization is the use of *affirmations* to create positive outcomes. It is an extremely dynamic technique because language has so much influence on our behavior. An affirmation is the use of strong, positive language in a way that makes "firm" that which you are visualizing. The process is so important that it warrants a chapter by itself. See Chapter 13 on The Language of Success.

As you begin to grasp the concept of visualization, the exercises throughout other chapters in this book will become second nature; the application of visualization to every aspect of your life will reward you with favorable outcomes. Caution in the use of visualization is advised in the following situations: first of all, it is only effective when used for the good of all. In other words, it cannot be used to harm others or bring about destruction in their lives; what you put out, you'll get back. Concentrate only upon bringing out what's best for each situation. Rather than imagine your opposition getting injured before a race, see yourself running well, forcing all those around you to perform up to their best. You may want to practice saying, "This, or something better, now manifests for me for the highest good of all concerned."

In addition to this, you must realize that what you visualize may not materialize. Rather than conclude that the technique is ineffective, examine the nature of your desires. You may be visualizing for something that is against your better interests without even knowing it. Part of yourself may be in opposition to the desires, the reason not being understood until much later. Have you ever really wanted something to happen only to realize in the future that not getting it was "a blessing in disguise?" When you visualize, just let it be and assume that the best will happen. In *Creative Visualization*, Gawain calls it "going with the flow." It's an ancient Chinese Taoistic philosophy which encourages you to hold onto your dreams, but lightly. Be willing to change them if something more important or rewarding comes into your life. You may have been rehearsing a certain time for the marathon over the past year when a marvelous opportunity comes your way, taking time away from the rigid running schedule. You run the race, only to fall short of your rehearsed goal. At this point, understand that on some level, your choice was to focus more on the new opportunity. Say to yourself, "Relax and let go, I can go with the flow." Becoming conscious about not achieving the original goal, paradoxically, will interfere with its ultimate attainment. Be firm in your pursuit, yet flexible in the outcome. Perhaps life is trying to tell you something.

Remember, in the game of visualization, you are the producer, director, writer and actor of all your imagined scripts. Enjoy the show! The following poem by Himne Ilili tells the story:

> Life is like a motion picture,
> a technicolor dream,
> and through your eyes the camera is
> projecting scene on scene.
> The plot unfolds both night and day.
> Sometimes you're lost, then you find your way.
>
> So follow your star.
> The star you are in the great big movie
> of your mind.

4

Desire and passion, more than talent, are the essential ingredients for achieving high levels of excellence. Performance in sport is directly related to the amount of time and effort one is willing to expend in realizing the objectives . . . this is what commitment is all about.

**H. Cheng
(Chinese philosopher—
runner)**

Commitment:
The Mirror of Performance

Have you ever taken a vow or an oath, made a sacred pledge, received a warranty or publicly declared an intention? This is serious business, not to be taken lightly. Such is the nature of commitment as you strongly affirm the intention to follow through with established goals. In the next chapter, you will become more familiar with the process of goal setting, yet it will serve no purpose if the crucial factor in achieving your goal is absent. That factor is commitment, the conscious choice to *desire* the objective and the decision to devote the necessary time and effort required for fulfillment of that goal.

The key to making that choice is to determine if you really *want* the goal. That's not easily determined. You may like to have it; it may be nice or enjoyable; but, do you *want* it? Is it worth the effort? Why do you want to achieve that goal? Is it important enough to warrant your commitment—devotion to its realization above all else? To help determine the extent to which you *want* something, try taking a loss-gain inventory. In one column, list what you expect to lose by "going for it." Next to that, record what you expect to gain. Include the effects of such a decision on family and friends. Honest responses to this exercise will help clarify your situation and facilitate the decision as to whether or not commitment is feasible. You should give this exercise at least five days and record your thoughts as they develop. You may discover that there are more important aspects to life than running a sub-three hour marathon. Perhaps you are quite able to accomplish the task, yet it might not be worth the time and effort. Knowing this should enable you to put your running into perspective: without commitment (and that's your choice), you will not be as competitive as you could be; your performance will never reflect your true ability, and that's to be expected. So there is no need to become

frustrated and disgusted with your sport when you perform errati-
cally. If and when the sub-three hour goal becomes your passion,
you will, with the help of proper goal setting, reach your objective.

The most talented master's runner with whom I have worked
with was constantly depressed because he had been unsuccessful in
achieving his goals for over two years. He had tremendous ability
but failed to see that his true commitments were to his job and family.
Training sessions would be missed as he worked overtime; morning
runs were out of the question because he was overtired from the
previous night's social activity. Confused and disappointed, he
decided to quit running only to become terribly depressed. After we
talked for a few therapy sessions, he realized how irrational it was
to expect top performance when his heart said no to what his head
thought was possible. Eventually, he committed to his work, family
and friends. He needed to give himself permission to simply run for
health; world age-group records would have to wait. Rather than
internalize his lackluster performances and get down on himself, he
began to realize that they were the result of a conscious choice. He
had the ability to do well, yet decided to channel his energy elsewhere.

I have also worked with athletes who have been clearly committed to their sport at the expense of family and job. In particular, I
recall an up-and-coming world class triathlete who decided that training five to eight hours a day was more important than his social,
professional or family life. As a matter of fact, his wife gave him an
ultimatum: "It's either me or your training." He opted for the latter
and now lives in a converted garage surrounded by sweaty clothes
and greasy chains. He has never regretted his move and seems quite
happy with his progress in his sport. He admits that the decision to
leave his wife and job was a painful one; what helped him to make
his choice was talking with friends and weighing the pros and cons
of not following his dream.

Sometimes the choice is clear and a decision as to where your
commitment lies will be easy to make. If there are several twinges
about which direction to go, I suggest taking all the time that's necessary to come to a resolution. Get people to help you explore options
and alternatives. The outcome need not be drastic and filled with
resentments and pain.

Commitment is essential if you're concerned with bringing out the best in that particular situation. Since the inception of the running craze, we have constantly searched for the magic potion to facilitate optimal performance. Proper diet, diminutive body size, the right shoe, carbo-loading, new training techniques and a host of other ingredients have helped, yet often overlooked is the importance of *commitment* in the runner's bag of tricks. Most elite marathoners that I have worked with agree that without it, all of the other ingredients combined would not get you to where you think you would like to go.

To demonstrate that one's level of commitment is fundamental to excellence in sport, I asked a group of elite and recreational runners to comment on their levels of commitment. On a scale of 1 to 10 (10 = "it's the most important thing to me"; 1 = "it's not very important to me."), they were asked to rate the importance of running in their lives. The elite group (recorded marathon times of 2:10 to 2:18) responded with 8's, 9's and 10's. Those with the fastest race times across the board had scored consistently higher than those who were slower. As the level of commitment decreased, so did the performance. The exact same pattern was revealed by the recreational athletes.

You may think you are committed, yet how can you be certain? There are numerous indicators that can help you to determine this. First of all, friends and relatives will no longer ask, "Did you run today?" "How far did you run?" will replace that statement, indicating their awareness of your commitment.

Experimenting with dietary changes, weight training and other allied fitness programs indicate the presence of a serious undertaking as well.

Many runners indicate that the ability to see setbacks as learning opportunities is a clear declaration of commitment. Those with little or no commitment see setbacks as justification to abandon their dreams. When used constructively, setbacks are educational tools allowing you to correct your course on the road to achieving your goals.

Other indicators of true commitment are: the insistence upon not using excuses for marginal performance; a view of competition as a force to help bring out your best; a thirst for new ways to improve; the ability to put forth extra effort when needed; the absence of lingering doubt, a willingness to stake everything on it; a refusal to see discouragement as anything but natural and an overall sense of joy and motivation toward your daily running routine.

If, at this point, you feel somewhat committed, perhaps you would like to measure the strength of your personal vow; the stronger the commitment, the more likely you are to reach your objectives. You can assess yourself by using the scale that follows developed by Terry Orlick, author of *In Pursuit of Excellence*, and adapted by myself for runners. The scale is a useful guide to help you become more aware of the requirements of high level excellence. Any score above 32 indicates that a sufficient level of commitment is present. Forty or higher says that your commitment is quite strong.

RATING SCALE

Commitment Conditions	Low Completely False		So-So	High Completely True
1. Willing to sacrifice other things to excel in the sport	1	2	3	4 5
2. Really want to become an outstanding runner	1	2	3	4 5
3. Never let up or give up in a race	1	2	3	4 5
4. Work hard to correct mistakes from past events	1	2	3	4 5
5. Give 100% effort when needed	1	2	3	4 5
6. Train during all weather conditions	1	2	3	4 5
7. Put in extra time preparing for big events	1	2	3	4 5

8.	Push hard even when it hurts (race or training)	1	2	3	4	5
9.	Feel more committed to improvement in running than anything else	1	2	3	4	5
10.	Feel more successful or gain more recognition in running than anything else	1	2	3	4	5

I administered this scale to the same 20 athletes mentioned before. The 10 elite marathoners had total scores that averaged 41. The 10 club members scored slightly lower, as expected, for an average of 36. Interestingly enough, when I ranked the total of 20 according to commitment scores, it turned out that those with the highest score had the fastest marathon times as well. It's important to understand that your total is not a blueprint boxing you in for life. You can raise your score on any item which should consequently increase your level of performance. Use the scale to become aware of those areas where work needs to be done.

Work on raising the score and developing a higher level of commitment. It's not as difficult as it may appear. If you have the passion and desire to do so, there are ways to accomplish this. First of all, start with writing a contract to declare your intentions. For example, "I will give 100 percent effort" or "I will train in all weather conditions" are ways to specify your intentions. Put your signature on the contract and post it where it will be highly visible each day. Such actions will serve as constant reminders of what must be done. You can certainly use the encouragement and inspiration from others which will help keep you honest and motivated. Secondly, your chances of success are greatly increased if *you* decide what's best for you, rather than letting others influence your decision. You know more than anyone else what that may be. Keep outside influences to a minimum. Determining your own path will increase the level of investment in your goal. Thirdly, the use of affirmations (see chapter on The Language of Success) will help to reinforce your level of

commitment. In a relaxed state, repeat over and over, the following phrases, or ones like them: "I (your name) am totally committed to running excellence"; "I (your name) am strongly committed to running a marathon." Your mind is most receptive to such suggestions; such powerful statements will be interpreted by the central nervous sytem as being real. Be sure to "see" yourself as committed. (See Chapter 3 on Visualization.)

At this point, you should determine how best to use the next chapter: Going for the Goal. With your commitment in focus, you are now ready to constructively set goals for super-performance. It will be helpful to keep goals clear, concise, realistic, challenging and reachable within the near future.

It is important to realize once again that not reaching a goal may have more to do with your level of commitment, rather than how good a runner you are. Without true commitment, your level of performance will consistently fall short of your abilities. Perhaps you should think about adjusting those expectations; would it be fine to finish refreshed or just go the distance? Concentrate on other aspects of your life where you truly are committed, and give yourself the strokes that you deserve for reaching those goals.

Lighten up on yourself and refrain from judging your athletic abilities as inferior. After all, considering the amount of time you now devote to running, you may be doing quite well. The bottom line is that performance in any area of endeavor is determined by

how much effort is expended. Your level of commitment, if very strong, will allow you to develop your true abilities. If the commitment is not there, that performance will fall short of what would normally be possible. Remember that anything which is truly important to you in life is worthy of your total commitment. Goals, once thought impossible to reach, become free of impenetrable barricades. Once commitment is established, you deserve to attain those goals.

As you begin the next chapter, I would like to relate to you a quote I once read years ago that helped create movement in my life:

> Until one is committed, there is hesitancy, the chance to draw back . . . concerning all acts of initiative there is one elementary truth—the ignorance of which kills countless and splendid plans: that the moment one definitely commits oneself, then providence moves too.

5

The deepest personal defeat suffered by human beings is constituted by the difference between what one was capable of becoming and what one has become.

Ashley Montagu

Going for the Goal: Personalized Plans for Progress

It has been said that the direction in which you as a runner are going is more important than where you stand at the moment. Perhaps you have been logging the miles for a few years and the only observable improvement is how better you've become at getting disappointed, frustrated and unmotivated with running. Standing here, in this moment, analyzing and regretting the past with its unrewarding, dogged pursuit for achievement, will only contribute to your frustration with goals unobtained. For you, I have three words: *analysis is paralysis*.

Goal direction today is the first step toward the creation of a successful running future. The establishment of objectives in a creative fashion is perhaps the most powerful force for personal improvement and motivation. Although your progress in any endeavor is a function of clearly defined, realistic and challenging goals, there must certainly be present a passionate commitment to pursue those objectives.

My work with elite marathoners at the U.S. Olympic Training Center and experience as a competitive distance runner has helped me to realize that the difference between those who reach their goals and those who fall short can be attributed to their level of commitment; the stronger the commitment, the better their chances for obtaining objectives. I see this trend with recreational-competitive runners as well. They complain about not reaching their goals; either they are unrealistic in their desires or simply not committed to the goal. Perhaps other aspects of their life are more important yet they don't realize it. If the job, family or other worthwhile endeavors are more important, then running goals should and will take a back seat— for now. Admitting this to yourself will help relieve the frustration and disappointment with an activity like running that you thought was most important. The *key* in this situation is to choose your priorities carefully and create your goals accordingly.

Whatever you choose is what you'll get (assuming the goal-setting process is properly carried out). Respect your decision, as that choice is indicative of your true needs. Albert Einstein had some healthy advice when he emphatically stated that "we must learn to differentiate clearly the fundamentally important, that which is really basic, from that which is dispensable, and to turn aside from everything else, from the multitude of things which clutter up the mind and divert it from the essential." Such is the true nature of commitment. (For more on commitment, read Chapter 4.)

If you feel particularly certain about your commitment to progress and improvement with running, you are ready to establish concrete, realistic goals. What is a goal? *Webster's Dictionary* uses the term interchangeably with the word *objective*. A goal is like the rudder of a ship, giving you direction when the sea of obstacles—injury, fatigue and other setbacks—stand in the pathway of progress. Goals are like dreams or mental images that one chooses to act upon. Joan Benoit had a dream; her goal was "to go for the gold" in the 1984 Olympic marathon. Through the process of constructive goal setting, her dream came true. Carl Lewis made his goals quite clear: to win four gold medals at the XXIII Olympiad. Had he wanted the world record in the long jump as well, he would have made that his goal; perhaps he saw the possibility of that interfering with his primary objective and wisely decided, much to the chagrin of the spectators, to forego the attempt. One of the hallmarks of a true champion is to disregard the opinion and wishes of the masses unless it fits into his/her plan; you must go for your goal unrelentingly, regardless of what others may think. Athletes who understand the science of goal setting reach their destination. Those who don't fall short, only to experience frustration and disappointment throughout their athletic careers. You can be one of those who understands by incorporating the following suggestions into your training regimen.

Goals, first of all, can be long term investments or immediate short term concerns. Usually, the long term objectives are the guiding mechanisms for the short range type. For example, Charles Lindbergh had a long range goal of piloting a plane on the first solo transatlantic flight. This guiding mechanism enabled him to plan for fuel conservation; celestial navigation; what and how to eat; how to stay awake and a host of many other short term objectives. In your world of running, you may follow a similar plan. Wishing to complete a sub-three hour and 30 minute marathon will require many short term goals: speed workouts, LSD workouts, proper dietary measures, a certain speed for a 10-kilometer race, completing a certain number of specific races; the list goes on and on. The successful completion of each short range goal establishes the confidence you will need to achieve the major objective. Motivation to continue toward your goal will result from all those quick, small successes. They will establish momentum and become symbolic suggestions to

your subconscious which facilitates the achievement of your major goal of 3:29 or better. When you establish this long term goal, shelve it and get on with the more immediate objectives; focusing on long term goals could get discouraging as success and satisfaction are delayed. Those small "victories" will also widen your horizon; goals that yesterday seemed difficult to achieve will become more plausible because of the success experienced by obtaining short term objectives.

If you divide your marathon training program into three distinct manageable segments—stamina, strength and speed—you'll be able to establish many simple goals. For instance, stamina can be achieved by running miles and miles. Perhaps you want to run 75 miles per week for six to eight weeks. Strength means to add hill workouts. Speed involves cutting back mileage and doing quality track and racing workouts. Each has a specific purpose; gear your goals for that purpose. Each week of each phase requires the setting of goals, all directed toward the final objective of a 3:29 marathon or better.

How about that time? Is it too ambitious? Do you wonder how high you should set goals? How do you establish a goal that is both realistic and challenging? I have found the following guidelines to be helpful to athletes of all abilities.

GUIDELINES FOR SUCCESSFUL GOAL-SETTING

1. It is crucial to be honest in evaluating your abilities as an athlete. I want to establish *realistic* goals to avoid the crushing feelings of failure, frustration and disappointment. Yet, I don't want to sell myself short in the process. I find that my real limits are usually beyond what I can even imagine. There is often a wide gap between my *real limits* and those that I believe to be my limits. I need to examine what I think are my limits and go beyond them. In assessing my limits, I need to choose goals that are in concert with my lifestyle. Working 60 hours per week would certainly interfere with running nationally competitive times, regardless of my physical attributes. Perhaps the time to train is available, yet the physical components are in short supply. At 132 pounds, I should not entertain the possibility of playing right tackle for the New York Giants. In any event, talk to a runner friend, spouse or coach—someone who can help you

to assess your abilities. Based on your workouts and short race performances, you may be surprised to know that you are underestimating your abilities or overestimating the difficulty of the event.

At a recent pre-race seminar of mine, a participant asked if his goal for the marathon was realistic. He wanted to run a 2:55, having already completed one in 2:59:17. After reviewing his training log and 10K times, I felt he was being a bit conservative. Four weeks prior to our conversation, he had run a 35:31, 10K. (Most race prediction charts indicate that such a time translates into a 2:47+ marathon.) It has been said that "What you can conceive you can achieve." If you feel that it's possible, go for it and, in time, it will be reached. Of course, the evidence must indicate that it is possible. I decided to explore this with him. I asked him, "How about 2:35?" "No way" he exclaimed. "Well, then 2:40?" "Not quite yet" he hesitantly replied. (This hesitation is a cue that a realistic goal is being approached.) I then suggested a 2:45, which drew a quick "maybe." He seemed ready to explore a new horizon. When I suggested a 2:48, he said "under perfect conditions, I could probably do that." He pointed out his fear of setting that up as a goal and I suggested that, instead, he choose a range within which success would be realized. He promised to visualize the possibility of a 2:46 to 2:55 for the upcoming marathon. I needed for him to affirm this because if he was on a 2:48 pace at mile 18, he wouldn't panic—it was within the range. If he was on a 2:55 pace, that would also be acceptable. Three weeks after that race, I received a postcard. All it said was, "Incredible— 2:47:36—how can I thank you enough?"

You can try this process on yourself. Choose a time that is 7 percent faster than what you *know* you can run at this point. That new time will appear unreasonable, so start counting back as I did above. The very moment you can say, "I can see that happening" or "it's possible," *stop*—this is your new realistic range. Be sure to see it as a range to allow for the unexpected happening. A 2:30 marathoner will have a range from 2:20:50 to 2:30. I'll bet that a 2:27:34 sounds realistic. "Go for it" in your visualization and training. Mentally gear yourself for that eventuality. As Henry Ford once said, "Whether you think you can or you think you can't, you're probably right." If you fail to reach the new goal right away, don't despair. Patience and persistence will enable you to arrive.

2.   Now that you are on target with realistic, achievable goals, consider whether they are *challenging and compelling*. Many runners complain about the lack of motivation; in addition, the satisfaction of achieving objectives that require hard work is enormous. To what degree does a runner's love affair with the marathon revolve around the strange pleasure of overcoming the challenge it offers? There are a multitude of variables that one must address to run successfully— dietary considerations, sleep and rest, mental preparation, course selection, time of the year and weather probabilities are but a few.

How do you determine if a goal is challenging? Simply use your *intuition*. Ask yourself the question, "How challenging is it?"; the answer, of course, should allow for *realism* as previously discussed. It is true that a transcontinental run is challenging, yet it may not be *realistic*. You must choose objectives that you intuitively feel are challenging. You may be "winning" your age division at local races where there exists a dearth of competition. It serves a purpose, yet quickly becomes boring and motivation and optimal performance will suffer. To realize your potential and improve, you may want to consider testing your abilities in a more challenging environment. You may not "win"—but you will be pushed to your optimum. If you honestly fear failure, be assured that these are legitimate feelings and the best of athletes have struggled with this. I refer you to the chapter on Fear of Failure for a broader perspective on this issue.

You may also try to solicit, once again, the opinions of a coach, or those who know you well, for a better understanding of what would be challenging to you. The final decision, of course, must be yours, but their perceptions may reinforce what you already believed, yet questioned about yourself, and be a source of confidence so necessary to take on the task.

3. The next step, following the establishment of realistic, challenging objectives, is the evaluation of your progress toward the goal. This is crucial. In order for progress to be measured, objectives must be *specifically stated;* specific race times, specific number of workouts per week and specific number of miles run for a given period are examples of assessment. In your mind's eye, "see" the time registered on your watch or digital recorder as you cross the finish line—2:43:17. Perhaps your workout goal will be 55 miles in seven sessions; one of the speed sessions may be a 5-mile "tempo"

run in 35 minutes. Whatever the goal, be as specific as possible. I strongly encourage runners to draw up a weekly contract, sign it and post it in a conspicuous place. It doesn't have to be complicated: "I will accomplish _____ by _____" is a workable format. You may want to use a chart to record progress toward your objective. It is quite rewarding to watch a line graph rise as you accomplish the task. It is a quick, visual method that gives instant feedback. Become artistic and creative by color-coding each goal. This adds to the enjoyment.

4. You're all set. Realistic, challenging and specific goals have been created. With *patience and persistence* they will be realized. Although delay of gratification is difficult to contend with, if you get up just one more time than you fall, you will be rewarded for your persistence. A steam engine's effort to pull 100 cars at a water temperature of 211° is futile. One more measly degree of heat (the boiling temperature of water is 212° F.) will enable that same engine to barrel up and over a mountain pass lugging a century of coal cars behind it. What if it quit after reaching the 211 degrees? Sometimes all you need for a major breakthrough in your performance is "one more degree" of persistence.

Improvement through goal-setting is also a process of trial and error; such a process is time-consuming and demands much patience. Two steps forward and one back will eventually get you to your destination. Being impatient, however, can actually interefere with goal attainment. To be impatient is to create stress which directly inhibits the natural fluidity of your muscles, thus preventing you from performing optimally. This happened with an elite athlete I worked with from a major west coast university. He wanted to run 27:50 for 10K on the track—*now!* He raced often—too often perhaps—only to become terribly frustrated and disappointed, never being able to do better than 28:03. He impatiently pushed harder in his workouts in order to get better until finally, tired of waiting, tired of training, he decided two weeks before the NCAA championships to run under 28 minutes in a regional track meet. The pressure, tension and stress mounted and played havoc with his body until, three days before the race, he severely injured his right Achilles tendon. Relieved, in a strange way, from the pressure he had created, he decided to shelve his efforts and back off his obsession. We talked often during this "down time" as he struggled to understand his dilemma. He began to see how his impatience and unwillingness to delay gratification contributed to his stress, which ultimately caused tension in his musculoskeletal system, setting the stage for injury. Following a four-week layoff, he came back rejuvenated with a new perspective on the matter. Within three weeks, in the absence of self-induced pressure, he clocked a magnificent 27:46. Like the elusive butterfly, you can chase one for hours and come up empty-handed. Lay down in the field, be patient and one will probably land on your nose.

Since the goal-setting process is one of trial and error, you must remember that setbacks are to be expected; they are a natural consequence of taking a risk and trying to improve. They are temporary, however, and are actually opportunities to learn and re-evaluate our situation and go on from there. With new data from the setback—"I went out too fast"; "I surged too early"; "I overtrained and ran tired"—you can re-establish new goals and proceed accordingly with the updated information. I have known of runners who ran a series of progressively slower races prior to a major personal best. Once again, I make reference to Olympic gold medalist, Joan Benoit. Prior to her 1983 Boston Marathon victory, she ran a series of marathons ranging from 2:30 to 2:37, each one slower than the previous attempt; this would discourage the best of us. But not Joan. Learning from each experience, she proceeded according to the data, running a splendid world record performance that year in Boston in 2:22:43. By the way, her near-suicidal pace (5:27 per mile) would have won every Olympic marathon up to 1960.

What if you reach your goal sooner than expected? Perhaps you are underestimating your ability or overestimating the difficulty of the task. Reset your goals and move on to broader horizons. If this should occur too often, you probably need to reassess the situation. Are you purposely avoiding challenging tasks? Are you out of touch with your level of skill? In any event, know that you are well capable of more at this stage of your training.

USEFUL SUPPORT SYSTEMS FOR GOAL REALIZATION

Now that you have a clearer picture of the goal-setting process, you may want to consider a number of support systems useful in sustaining movement toward the obtaining of these objectives. The list, although not exhaustive, can be most useful when you experience a physiological or psychological lull in your training. The road to your destination is often a lonely one with many obstacles. The following strategies may "help you through the night."

1. *Incorporate Your Goals.* Perhaps you are a runner and an amateur photographer and your husband loves to travel. You have two children and wish to spend quality time with them. Why not plan a trip to "Grandma's Marathon" (or some other fun race if you happen to live in Duluth), bring the family and take some good photos of the Badlands, Mt. Rushmore and other points of interest. The kids will be out of school in June and the swimming and boating in northern Minnesota is wonderful this time of year. Such combining of goals into one project can bring a sense of joy and fulfillment to all involved. Altruistically or not, the family will support your efforts all the way. The possibilities are limitless. How about the London Marathon?

2. *Get a "Goal Buddy."* Aside from the family support, try to get someone of equal ability to share your goal. With mutual objectives, you can be an endless source of encouragement and inspiration for each other; you could spur one another on when discouragement sets in. Your workouts together will become more enjoyable, particularly those that require hard track efforts or those long, lonely distance sojourns. Improvement will be rapid as each of you will invariably alternate pushing each other to run a bit faster than planned. Such an arrangement plays into your competitive nature and helps to "bring out the best."

3. *Build Fun into the Program.* The process of training and goal attainment must be fun and enjoyable, otherwise it will cease. Concentrating on the outcome or product (the goal itself) alone, interferes with the joy and the pleasure of the process. As Alan Watts once said, "We don't sing (just) to get to the end of the song . . . we don't dance to get from one place on the floor to another." The process on the road to a goal is, indeed, something to behold. Perhaps one of your goals could be to enjoy the workout; a run in the forest with a friend, followed by breakfast, could be a wonderful way to start the day. If you do mile repeats for your track workouts, try alter-

nating leads for each lap with your buddy; see if each of you can run exact splits. Be creative and let the imagination run as wild as you. A wonderful byproduct of such creativity is the maintenance of motivation and greater control over the "running doldrums."

4.   *Visualize Your Goal*. One of the strongest support systems you have is your mind's eye. Clearly see yourself reaching your goal and experience in your mind how that would feel. (See Chapter 3.) The clearer your imagery and picture of achievement, the easier it is to accomplish the task. Remember that the central nervous system does not distinguish between a real or imagined event; your body will follow the images as if they were real. I have seen athletes hooked up to an electromyograph machine (a device that measures muscle response and activity) and, in a deep relaxed state, told to visualize running up and down a hill. With the athletes resting in a "sleep state" on a table, the graph recorded movement of those muscles

necessary for climbing and descending hills; they responded simply to the images alone. Apply the concept of visual imagery to your goals and you will have strong support in your attainment of those objectives. Remember—"What you see is what you get."

5. *Develop Self-Affirmation.* Affirmations are short, concise imagery phrases which, when repeated often enough, create the clarity and confidence you need to reach your goals. A few examples would be—"Lean and trim, I run to win"; "Silky, smooth and swift, I run to get a lift"; "Everyday, in every way, I excel and run well." The body is extremely suggestive and receptive to such images. Create your own self-suggestions. In a relaxed state of mind, repeat the phrase over and over. The statement should be one that you believe about yourself or you will become in the future. State it as if it were already true. Choose only those ideas that are possible for you even if they haven't been realized. (See Chapter on The Language of Success.)

The question often arises, is it better to announce my goals or should they be kept secret? Whatever makes you feel most comfortable is my usual reply. For some runners, there is a risk of experiencing anxiety and undue pressure once the goal is publicized. Such stress will interfere with your performance. In addition to that, once announced, your goals will be subject to the scrutiny of your peers; there will be the barrage of questions when you return from the race: "What was your time?"; "Did you place?" This could be painful. I made the mistake of telling "the world" of my plans to run a PR at a National TAC championship race. With great expectations, and even greater pressure, I registered my first DNF, dropping out at mile 4 (10-kilometer race), totally exhausted, tight and feeling like a beached whale. I didn't want to come home again and face those questions. The thought of running a race in the future looked dismal at best. I needed five months away from competition. Some friends suggested that I jump back into it but, honestly, the mind would not permit it.

On the other hand, goal pronouncement can actually be helpful. If used wisely, it can strengthen commitment and motivation, as well as giving those who know your intentions a chance to rally around and support the effort. You must ultimately decide when it's good to let the secret out. My rule of thumb is—keep goals to myself unless I'm fairly certain and confident about the outcome.

Finally, failure to reach your goals is no reason for moaning. I have seen too many seasoned runners become depressed, withdraw from the race scene and act irritably with those they love as a result of unfulfilled goals. Rather than *act* (learn from mistakes and forge ahead), they *react* and become destructive to themselves and others. Begin to look at goals as simply wonderful, fun ways to test your limits and to learn how to stretch beyond what you thought was possible. You learn more from goals unrealized than from those easily attainable. Each setback, rather than a failure, is a signal which says: *Stop*—don't go any farther; take what you've learned and proceed ahead.

Also, don't overlook the importance of pleasure in the goal-striving process. The ultimate paradox is that you must be serious about your goals; however, if you lose the ability to have *fun* in the process, goal attainment will be difficult, if not impossible. When running ceases to be fun, I'll predict that you will stop doing it. So— no matter what direction you choose to go—be sure to enjoy yourself on the way.

6

Motivation should not be a struggle. To become such is simply a matter of answering the questions—What do you want, and how do you want it? Insight into these queries will change a scarcity of enthusiasm to an overflowing abundance.

**H. Cheng
(Chinese philosopher-runner)**

Running on Empty?: Mental Guides for Motivation

$\mathbf{A}$lthough one of the strongest psychological forces for motivation with running is the process of setting clearly defined, realistic goals (Chapter 5), there are certain periods when interest in this process is totally lost; you become "burnt out" from the constant need to fulfill those objectives and begin to "run on empty." You find yourself doing what you can do just to keep your *love* (running) alive. You simply lose all motivation as running becomes a pleasureless activity in the quest for physical and emotional health. Michael Bonet, in his *Signification du Sport*, clearly points out that motivation and interest in sport ceases rapidly if it doesn't bring pleasure.

Intellectually, you are aware of the physiological and psychological advantages of regular exercise, yet such knowledge alone is insufficient to motivate you through what you perceive to be an endless, boring experience where the only "pleasure" is the conclusion of the run. Boredom, loss of pleasure and lack of interest are mental states that, indeed, are the greatest obstacles in the way of your ability to maintain consistent, year-round training, barring injury, of course. Therefore, is it possible and even advisable to maintain motivation throughout the year? If so, how is this best accomplished?

In answering the first question—*yes*, it is possible, yet breaks in the routine are highly recommended. For example, try to establish a wide variety of objectives throughout the year. If you try to be "up" at all times for racing, motivation will surely diminish. You could divide the year into a number of seasons; stamina season could be accomplished by just putting in those miles; then get excited about building strength, followed by a productive race season. When your racing has peaked out, motivate yourself to taking a short rest while

77

you get hungry for building your base once again. In this way, year-long motivation is very possible, although there will be times when getting out of that door will be difficult as you experience short term loss of interest.

This brings up the second question—how is motivation acquired during those "running on empty" moments? To begin with, the concept of motivation is somewhat intangible, being strongly influenced by various personal, societal, material and situational factors. Also, from a psychological point of view, it is difficult to explain the varying levels of motivation between individuals. All runners do not participate for the same motives: one person's candy is another's poison. It is safe to say, however, that most of us are motivated by intrinsic and/or extrinsic variables, all of which are related, on some level, to the *mind*. *If the mind* wants to run, for whatever reason, the body will, indeed, run. Later in this chapter, I will discuss various ways to raise your level of interest and pleasure in order to get through those arduous periods of boredom.

Why does a runner lose interest or become bored with an activity that had meant so much for so many months or years? I'm sure you can fill in the blank, "Whatever became of _____ ?" with the names of many elite or local runners. Check the race results from three years ago and see how many top runners have dropped out of the competitive spotlight. For one thing, high mileage, week after week, catches up with the best of us. If injury doesn't affect your motivation, then mental fatigue certainly will. Pounding the roads each day is, quite frankly, boring. Many neophytes to the sport can't get enough of their addiction to running and "burn out" emotionally. I know of a 40-year-old who, after only six months of running, began to take to the roads twice a day to get his mileage up. He did his second workout at night in front of a friend's car on the side of the road as the lights shined the way. After a few months of this routine, he quit suddenly and did not run a step for the next eight months. After his long hiatus, I saw him on the track where he told me he is only running four times a week and is very excited. He was fortunate enough to have learned from his radical running behavior.

Another reason why motivation is lost has much to do with how much ego-involvement one has invested in the sport. If you have a tendency to measure your self-worth by the outcome of your running, you will set yourself up for failure. You can't always do well and, as a result, the activity becomes a very dangerous mechanism for ego-deflation; you begin to avoid such situations when performance is down and motivation drops drastically. No one wants to experience the pressure of constantly having to live up to unrealistic expectations of "being on." Such runners tend to be externally motivated, measuring success by society's standards rather than by their own inner rewards. External motivators are fine, but if that's all there is, pleasure and interest rapidly dwindle when the bucks or trophies cease to exist. In our society, there is an exaggerated emphasis on the importance of external reward which sets the stage for possible "burn-out." Ideally, you should have a delicate balance between external and internal motivating factors to enable the flame of enthusiasm to shine for extended periods of time. More on this later.

Like anything else in life, motivation is lost if you repeat the same activity over and over—year in and year out—with little or no variation. Variety is the spice of life as well as motivation. Even an eight-month-old infant needs a mixture of activities to maintain

interest and attention. Within your job of 20 years, timely changes have kept you going; changes in your marriage over the years have enabled you to maintain the interest and excitement needed to sustain the relationship. So it is with sports. Many runners are discovering their long-held love for a new relationship because for years, they ran each day with little or no variation. The excitement is gone. Witness the participation in the triathlon boom as runners are searching for something new. Athletes need and crave change within their sport or they will seek pleasure elsewhere. Mentally, change creates excitement and rejuvenates your enthusiasm.

Most of all, loss of interest and motivation can be best attributed to the anhedonic (absence of pleasure) nature of training regimens. Quite simply, where is the fun of the run? There is none? "Seriousness" is epidemic in the running community. The attitude I feel from runners with "long faces" as we pass on the run in opposite directions is: "This is serious business. I'm training for a marathon. It hurts and I'm in pain and there's no time to smile." It's as if they feel they couldn't possibly be working hard enough. Anything worthwhile must be difficult. It's the old work ethic once again. Little do they know that frowning creates tension throughout the entire body and such stress makes one tired. There needs to be more joy experienced while *on the run*, not just when it's over. Runners tend to be rather spartan about having fun and their social life goes on hold. If your motivation is low, perhaps there's a paucity of *fun* in your training program. I always said that when running is no longer a joy, I would quit out of choice. I make sure to build into my life of motion, enjoyable episodes and experiences. Many ex-runners' major complaint is that it ceased to be enjoyable. Fred Rohé, in his book, *The Zen of Running*, captured the essence of this feeling when he said,

> . . . if the dance of the run isn't fun
> then discover another dance, because
> without fun the good of the run
> is undone, and a suffering runner
> always quits, sooner or later.

Having looked at some of the factors that contribute to a loss of interest, what are some of the variables that could possibly strengthen your motivation to run? Generally, motivation can be external or internal, or a combination of both. Recognition by a coach, friends or family; attention through the media; prize money, medals, trophies and trips; promotional contracts and job offers, are ways to give athletes what they want and, in this sense, are external motivators. The built-in danger associated with these rewards is their ephemeral nature and the dependency they create on outside forces. Because of this, it is important to develop a sense of internal reward to enhance self-reliance during those times when the external recognition is not easily available. Intrinsic variables include the positive emotional feelings generated by the run; physiological benefits experienced as a result of exercise; optimal levels of arousal that can be had; feelings of exhilaration and euphoria; development of self-respect and acceptance and the possibility of discovering who you are in all your uniqueness. Such motivators are determined by each athlete on an individual, personal basis. I personally feel that the intrinsic rewards are the most powerful and lasting. The introduction of big-time, corporate participation coupled with prizes 10 deep in age categories broken into 5-year segments, was supposed to motivate people to participate in the race scene. Paradoxically, such strategies have taken the emphasis away from why we run in the first place; these factors also create deleterious effects on performance as they fractionate the athletic energy in all directions with little left for proper *focusing* on the event. I see a need for a delicate balance between internal and external reward.

It is my wish that every one of you maintain a level of motivation that will keep you going. I have much to gain when you're running well—the world is a better place today because people are generally more fit and, therefore, more pleasant and happier. My positive addiction has powerful repercussions on my work and relationships with people. When the motivation is low, I don't run well (if at all) and, I'm sorry to say, everything else seems to be affected. During such times, I need to recall the reasons why running is so important in my life. The following strategies I have found to be helpful to me and other athletes when there was a need to enhance interest and motivation for my favorite activity:

1. *Become Affiliated*—Since recognition by others is a strong extrinsic motivator, I would suggest becoming affiliated with a

local running group or club. By so doing, you will meet other runners of your caliber, receive pertinent information about seminars and clinics and expand your social contacts as well. Knowing, for instance, that you're racing for a team will motivate you to maintain a higher level of fitness. Of course, be aware that there is a danger of feeling too much pressure to perform and this will contribute to "burn-out" and loss of motivation. Use the group to motivate you to do track workouts or run on a rainy day. Just knowing that they will be there will encourage you to get out of bed and show up. Most clubs have newsletters; this is one way of getting your name in print either through your race results or by your writing a column. Some clubs also have annual award ceremonies to recognize various runners' accomplishments throughout the year.

2. *Try Competition*—One of the easiest ways to motivate myself is to choose a race in the near future and try to peak for it. My

goal is to make it the race that I will run "out of my mind" as it all comes together. I usually have a backup race if things don't go according to schedule. If you want to experience a sense of accomplishment or knowledge of improvement, I would strongly suggest competition in the form of racing. You should remember that the pressure to achieve must not be so great so as to unmotivate you or remove the joy of participation. You want to test yourself to the point of seeing improvement and experiencing success. Through such efforts in competition, you will improve self-confidence and self-respect and subsequently increase your motivational level. Feedback is instantaneous. For starters, you may want to try a few of the low-keyed fun runs in your community. Then again, you may be more inclined to experience a production that includes 5000-6000 enthusiastic plodders. The sheer numbers alone may compel you to search for some kind of explanation as to why racing is that enjoyable. Dick Taylor, U.S. Olympic Biathlete, writes so poignantly about the contagious enthusiasm which has gripped cross-country skiers and road racers: "The race is a ritual, a highly compacted human experience situation . . . it is the measure of our curiosity about optimum human possibility . . . the sustenance coming from a shared sense that all are relatively more alive from having 'died' a little and well. The experience of expanded personal potential and relativity with other humans is both profound and rare . . . a deeper sense of belonging, to oneself and to a community. Self-confirmation happens simultaneously with a community venture . . . ultimately making a winner of everybody." "When is the next race" you ask. George Leonard, author of *The Ultimate Athlete*, once said that we must create environments where people have permission to use their natural powers. Competition is, indeed, one of those environments that will allow for this as well as enhance our intrinsic and extrinsic motivation.

3. *Use the "Hawthorne Effect"*—Another technique for increasing your motivational level is to make use of a psychological principle called the *Hawthorne Effect*. Simply stated, it means that any changes in routine or environment result in increased motivation, and, subsequently, increased performance. For example, many of you who are quite discouraged are probably running with a fixed, minimal repertoire of workouts in a repetitive fashion. Facing such boredom would test the most compulsive,

committed runner. According to the *Hawthorne Effect*, any
slight change in the regimen would sufficiently excite you to run
again. There are a multitude of possibilities. First of all, vary
your workouts. Rather than run your miles at the same pace each
day, change your speed: run slow for a while then switch to a
faster pace; run two short workouts today, one long one tomorrow; run alone today, tomorrow try it with a friend or group; try
some intervals for a workout; alternate walking and running and
see how far you can go before tiring; try running during different
times of the day; make the workout meaningful by aligning it to
one of your goals (running a faster 5 miles, for example). There
are endless combinations if you use your imagination. The possibilities become even more interesting if you vary the environment where you run, as well as the workout. Until you are
capable of running higher mileage, you may have to drive to
another location, but the rewards are worth it. Running on a
track every day is emotionally tiring and probably boring as
well. Try going up some hills. You'll probably run slower, but
the benefits will be greater and your enthusiasm will soar. If it's
hills today, do some roadwork tomorrow. If there are some well-
defined trails around, you and a friend may want to explore them
on the run. If you're visiting a friend in another town, bring
running gear and discover the area by going for a run after you
arrive. When you have a particularly good run, remember where
it was and return in a few days. You'll be amazed how exciting
it will feel to go back for more enjoyment. If you plan properly
the night before, you will find your motivation level quite high
as you look forward to a "new" workout. Finally, don't overlook
the possibility of a day off in your schedule as a technique to
increase your "hunger" for running. Regardless of your choice,
the more playful the sport becomes, the better your mental out-
look will be towards continuing your efforts. For example, try
leaving your watch at home and forget about recording miles.
Run home from the movies instead of walking or taking a bus.
Run to the Post Office when you need stamps. A favorite story
of mine is about a client who found it particularly motivating to
carry running gear wherever she went in case an opportunity
came her way to buy a few miles. On a trip from San Jose to
Denver, the plane stopped in Salt Lake City for a three-hour
layover. She quickly found the nearest women's room, jumped
in the stall, changed her clothes, and in Superwoman fashion

burst into a run like a speeding bullet, out of the airport and into the city. Her motivation to see Salt Lake City, as well as to get back in time for the flight, enabled her to have one of the fastest distance runs of her career. I wonder what she does while waiting for a table in a restaurant? By using your imagination, you'll discover endless ways of lessening the "work" of running and turning it into play.

4. *Consider Physiological Benefits*—Do not be deceived by the obvious simplicity of this exercise as it has been proven to be a very effective method in helping to motivate people into action. Simply listing the physiological benefits expected to be gained from running and posting it on the refrigerator door will help keep in perspective those important intrinsic reasons for continuing your efforts. The bottom line for why most of us begin and continue to run seems to be physiological in nature. Your dreams of a healthier, happier life must be kept alive and vivid. Some of the specific benefits you may wish to list are:

- *Lower blood pressure*—With regular exercise, you experience increased vessel size and elasticity, the major factors involved in decreased blood pressure.

- *Blood quality rises*—Through exercises, there is an increase in the number of blood cells, more hemoglobin and more plasma (the liquid portion of blood). Also, the blood's ability to dissolve clots will improve (called the "fibrinolytic response").

- *High-density lipoprotens levels rise*—HDLs apparently help clear the arteries of unhealthy cholesterol deposits. Regular aerobic exercise raises the level of HDLs in the blood, thus intensifying the cleansing process.

- *Heart gets stronger*—Like any muscle, the heart will grow larger and stronger if it's worked. Running regularly will help the heart to become more efficient and effective.

- *Lungs become more efficient*—When you stress the lungs through aerobic exercise, they open up and flush out, using more air space. Running helps to reduce the effects of asthma and emphysema.

- *Muscle tone improves*—Your body begins to look aesthetically more appealing as muscles take on better tone and definition.

- *Control of osteoporosis*—A condition resulting from a too severe decrease in bone density, causing weaker bones which results in fractures. Running and exercise seem to delay or even reverse this possibility.

- *Weight control*—Exercise speeds up metabolism, suppresses the appetite and burns fat.

- *Gastro-intestinal system*—The G.I. tract becomes more efficient as exercise increases the motility of the intestines.

- *Aging is delayed*—Although more research is needed, it seems as though the above benefits help runners to age less quickly than their sedentary counterparts.

- *Thought processes enhanced*—There are some studies that indicate improvement in decision-making capability in subjects who exercise vigorously and on a regular basis.

- *Promotes creativity*—Although highly subjective, some runners feel that their sport facilitates the flow of ideas and thoughts. Many a chapter in this book was conceived on the run.

- *Stress control*—Probably one of the most irrefutable physiological benefits of running is that it is one of the most satisfying means of stress reduction.

- *Reduction in chronic tiredness*—Exercise stimulates the circulatory system, transporting an abundance of oxygen which enables you to remain alert and awake.

- *Controls degenerative diseases*—Regular aerobic activity makes you less vulnerable to such diseases as diabetes, arthritis, cancer and heart failure.

Of course, running is not the panacea for creating the perfect health system; coupled with a good diet and supportive home and work environment, such exercise can promote excellent wellness. To increase motivation during the running "blahs," read this listing once a day; your movement to the front door will replace your movement to the cupboard door.

5. *Reality-Check the Body*—Very often, it's difficult to motivate yourself to run because you feel tired after a full day's work. The fatigue you experience may very well be mental—you've been using the brain for hours. I find that once I get going, my body comes alive. If the thought of running 5 or more miles

seems overwhelming during these moments, make an agreement with yourself; just run for four minutes and, if things aren't looking better, turn around and run home. By the time you reach the door, you will have completed a mile, more or less; if the "fatigue" has been shaken, keep going. If not, you can write it off, stay inside, and use this time to stretch, read and relax; tomorrow's another day. Your body needs the break.

6. *Set the Stage for Success*—Many runners place unrealistic demands and set heroic expectation on their performance. This sets the stage for failure as they find themselves dreading the chore of following through on such promises. This is accompanied by a drop in motivation and increase in frustration; the desire to pursue any goals with running is eventually lost. Remember that if you keep the training program pleasurable and rewarding, interest will flourish. The success created as a result of reaching realistic expectations will enhance motivation.

7. *Substitute Alternative Methods*—Runners are beginning to discover that sports such as cycling and swimming enhance their fitness and give the legs a much deserved rest, as well as providing a psychological break from the running routine; this periodic rest from running contributes to the maintenance of a healthy level of motivation. World class athletes, like Jack Foster, have used the bike as an adjunct to their fitness program. Every Saturday, I find myself in a pool or on a bike, taking a break from the pounding out of miles. What I have learned inadvertently, is how that change increases my motivation to run on Sunday. By the way, a hard workout on a bike (hard is individually determined, of course) for 25 miles is the approximate equivalent of a strenuous 10-mile run, without the pounding (conversion factor is 2.5 to 1).

8. *Control Your Fears*—An increase in motivation may result from a concomitant decrease in the fears of success and failure. (See chapter on Fear of Success and Failure.) Many athletes, elite and recreational alike, choose to turn their backs on a challenge because of these fears, and the "rug of motivation" is subsequently pulled out from under them. If your motivation to compete has dwindled, perhaps you simply need a change of scenery. However, if you shy away from the races and you're not truly "burned out," take a close look at the possibility of a

phobia being present. The suggestions in the chapter on fears should be quite helpful in confronting these issues.

9. *Set Your Goals*—As stated in the first sentence of this chapter, goal-setting is recognized as possibly the strongest of all forces for personal motivation. It provides a sense of purpose and incentive propelling you to your destination in all kinds of weather. Beware, however, that goals need to be cautiously programmed; motivation will be strengthened as a result of successfully reaching your objectives. Follow the strategies in the chapter on Going for the Goal.

10. *Use Innovative Games*—As a high school basketball player, I loved going to practice because the coach would initiate a different, interesting game each day. The game was fun and it reinforced the skills he wanted to teach. Remembering this motivational technique, I create my own games when boredom sets in. For example, running along a 6-mile bike path that parallels a road, I try to guess the make and color of the car as it comes from behind; one point for each and a bonus if I get both. Running through the redwood forests in the Santa Cruz mountains allows me to trailblaze (discover new unmarked routes); it's exciting to find new areas to roam. When I'm really bored, I play the game of *lines*—the object is to never step on a crack in the road or on the sidewalk while maintaining stride. Be creative and invent a game of your own. If friends are available, the possibilities are limitless: follow the leader, tag, first one to the top of the hill are but a few alternatives. My favorite is to do mile repeats on the track with four people, alternating the lead at each quarter to see who can hit a predetermined split exactly as called.

11. *Stop Running*—When all else fails, back off completely. What have you got to lose; right now, you are becoming supersaturated and need a break. Remember the last time you ate a particular food every day until you became sick at the sight of it? Cooking it differently helped, but when you were totally disgusted with its mere presence, it was time to put it aside. When should you start in again after a layoff? The time to begin running is "when you get that feeling." Statements like "what a great day for a run" will give you a clue. The first three days are the most difficult as you experience the withdrawal syndrome. It gets easier each day after that as you discover how wonderful it is to have so much extra free time. My last "cold turkey" experience

lasted 18 days. I biked and swam only if I cared to and refused to read running books and magazines. On the 19th day, I remember getting an urge to run on the beach. I followed that craving and enjoyed every step of the run. Three days later I entered a crazy mountain race (no pressure as the distance was 5.83 miles and the terrain was vicious) and ran a faster time than I had two years previously on the same course. I do think that the bike helped, as well as having a relaxed mental framework.

Although listed individually, you will find that many of these motivational strategies overlap and reinforce each other. For example, becoming affiliated, competing, creating changes in your training, setting goals while also considering the physiological benefits from the sport, all interact to create a powerful level of motivation. The key is to try initiating those factors that are absent when interest is low. Remember that if you want to increase your level of motivation, if you become too intense or too serious, other problems will arise comparable to severe burn-out. If you find that you take yourself too seriously, lighten up and have a good time. The amount of enjoyment in running is limited only by your imagination. Keeping perspective on how you feel, your attitudes and values and your state of mind will prove to be very important to your motivation and success in running.

7

Most of us find something frightening about surpassing our own or others' expectations, and this *fear* usually keeps us from doing it. We identify with these expectations, and don't like to rock the boat by exceeding them.

**Timothy Gallwey
(author of *The Inner Game of Tennis)***

The Self-Limiting Double Bind: Fear of Failure and Success

$\mathbf{T}$he basic question raised by this insightful intro-
ductory quote is the crux of a confusing, subtle, double bind that all
of us so powerfully experience. What could be so terrribly frightening
about going beyond self-imposed limitations and experiencing the
athlete's dream—success? Isn't success something that we await with
open arms? Not necessarily! It appears that *fear of success* is a multifaceted emotion reaching epidemic proportions in the running community; there seem to be many frightening reasons why we stop short
of success. Strangely enough, one of the more obvious reasons is the
fear of failure. After all, "nothing recedes like success"; once success
has been obtained, anything short of that could be looked upon as
failure, something we abhor. Also, the pressure to uphold a reputation of being successful is enough to keep the best of us from "going
for it."

This chapter will attempt to untangle the intricacies of these
phobias and help you to go beyond their powerful influence. They
have had a limiting hold on many an athlete for too long; it's now
time to put these nasty goblins into perspective. Although they represent the most ubiquitous of psychological self-limited phenomena
(not an athlete seems to be spared), with a little work, you will emerge
victorious over their grasp and open the gates to improved performance.

FEAR OF FAILURE

During a recent conversation with one of my clients, it was
brought to my attention that his 10-year-old daughter had expressed
great fear and apprehension about her participation in an upcoming
sporting event. Upon hearing her concerns, he immediately reassured
her that there was no need to worry about where she placed; it didn't

matter to him. Simply taking the risk, participating and having fun in the process were truer indicators of success. With her "fear of failure" put aside, she enterted the contest and thoroughly enjoyed an experience she'll always remember. She started to perform more effectively and feel better about herself.

Many of us, however, were not so fortunate to have had such an aware, understanding parent. The word *failure* often conjures up nasty memories of our youth when we experienced subtle pressures from our parents and coaches to win. Perhaps we chose not to run out of the catastrophic fear that we'd place last and be subjected to someone's disapproval or harsh ridicule. This easily happens to a child, particularly when compared to an older, more "perfect" sibling. Also, an "only child" may feel the burden of "doing it all" so as not to disappoint mom and dad. Parents are often guilty of pressing their children to excel out of a subconscious desire to live vicariously through the youngster's triumph. The Vince Lombardi Syndrome— "Winning isn't everything; it's the only thing," is exhibited by many coaches and parents. Such a mentality could be responsible for much of the inadequacy experienced by these children as they approach adulthood. The message is quite clear: failure is abominable; to be avoided whenever possible. Ironically enough, failure cannot be avoided and, more often than not, it is a necessary prerequisite to success. Instructive by nature, failure teaches us much more than our successes. We learn from our mistakes. So many of us feel that we can and should perform perfectly the first time we attempt a challenge. This is a totally irrational and mythological expectation, perpetuated unfairly by those who had significant input into our formative years. Mistakes are a crucial aspect to any process of growth and development. Studies indicate that highly successful, creative people have a higher than ordinary tolerance for errors, mistakes and failures. They are willing to learn from the setbacks and push through those temporary "schooling" experiences. Such people do not possess exceptional talent; it is their dogged pursuit of the goal, a strong desire, determination and courage to risk failure that inevitably leads them down the road to success. Failure is an integral part of this process. Understanding this is a major step in the direction of overcoming the fear itself. Their attitude seems to be a willingness to answer the question, "How good am I, really?" regardless of the outcome. They all agree that it's better to find out before it's too late and be forced to live with all the regrets.

To facilitate your journey through the fear of failure, try adapting and adopting one or any combination of the following strategies. They have been gathered from my research, reading and personal experiences and used successfully with experienced athletes, recreational and elite alike.

1. *Go to Running School:* If you needed to learn the art of archery to hunt for food in order to live, you would do so, step-by-step, in trial and error fashion. If a mistake was made in the process of learning, you'd seek advice to remedy the situation, go out and try again until you became proficient—no blame, no embarrassment, no failure. So why not view your running similarly? A race is like going to running school. It's an opportunity to learn new strategies and tactics for better performance. Dwelling on the outcome interferes with your collection of valuable, experimental data which could contribute to better performance in the future. The Chinese character for our word *crisis* has two distinct meanings. On the one hand it indicates *danger;* it also means *opportunity.* Out of every race crisis situation, there is an opportunity to improve if you look past the ephemeral, and often meaningless, outcome. Put aside your disappointing results (personal bests don't come often anyway), and look at how you ran the race. Perhaps it was a fantastic success with respect to even pacing; maybe you were tactically sharp. These are no small achievements and should be recognized as such. If a mistake was made by going out too slowly, how does that change future performance strategy? Ask youself the question, "What might I have done differently to run more effectively?" In a relaxed state, visualize the race and rerun it with the newly learned information. Remember to throw away the negative and introduce the positive. Hold on to all that worked well. In a recent half-marathon, where I fell short of my expected outcome goal by 90 seconds, I realized that I could have paced myself better. At the start, there was a stiff tail wind. I could have taken advantage of that by going out faster as less effort would have been required to run more quickly. Instead, I ran my usual opening pace quite comfortably, even effortlessly. At the turnaround, I headed back into the gale and was never able to make up those valu-

able minutes. I have since used this information to great advantage in an out-and-back 20-kilometer race. Each race seems to be a wonderland of knowledge—if I choose to see it that way.

Keep in mind that this exercise does not change the event or your memory of it. It will, however, change the negative images of that event and allow you to confront the same situation in the future with a positive mental framework.

2. *Practice Patience:* If one virtue were to be required of all athletes it should be *patience.* After a series of disappointments, it is crucial to give yourself a change; failures are common. Too many runners lose their desire when negative circumstances arise (your view of these circumstances as negative will change if you keep the first strategy in mind). Thomas Edison experienced numerous setbacks on the path to discovery; through all his disappointment and frustration, he finally did "see the light." More often than not, your action does not immediately lead to the result you desire. To interpret this to mean your training efforts are not working is premature and erroneous. Understand that a *time delay* often exists between the moment you initiate change and when results begin to occur. Patience is essential as the desired results of a new regimen need time to appear. The outcome immediately following your new program may be the result of your previous erratic training. Consider this example:

TIME DELAY

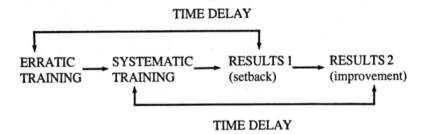

ERRATIC TRAINING → SYSTEMATIC TRAINING → RESULTS 1 (setback) → RESULTS 2 (improvement)

TIME DELAY

Result 1 is more indicative of the years of erratic, inconsistent training methods. Because it follows directly after your initiation of a more disciplined, systematic program, there is the danger of becoming *impatient* with your new training and casting it aside because it appears it is not working. You need to stick with it if Result 2 (improvement) is to be experienced. Remember that Olympian Joan

Benoit had a series of progressively slower marathons prior to her world record effort in Boston.

   3. *Will It Matter in Ten Years?:* When the outcome of an event is less than what you expected, put it into perspective by seeing what importance it has in the broad scope of life. What will it mean in ten years, or even one year for that matter? Another way to look at it is to ask the question, "What's the worst thing that could happen if, by chance, I fail?" If you can live with this "worst thing," I suggest that you "go for it." If it would be too devastating, wait for a more opportune time. In actuality, the answer to this question rarely is as catastrophic as we originally fantasized. As the achievement of success rarely lives up to one's greatest expectations, failure is never quite as devastating either. It is a feeling you experience at that moment. You are certainly disappointed, but the setback does not ring in your demise as an athlete.

4. *Performance is a Rollercoaster:* Some runners believe that they should be thoroughly competent, achieving and successful in all aspects of their sport at all times. Such thinking is extremely irrational and the cause of much severe athletic stress. Believing this myth may preclude participation in a race until you are totally ready and in the best of shape. Lighten up on yourself. It is impossible to set PRs every time you race. For every great 10K race you run, there will be another which leaves you dissatisfied. Most performances will fall somewhere in between the two extremes. Ups and downs are to be expected. Babe Ruth hit many homeruns in his career; he also struck out 1,333 times while trying. Many elite runners throughout the world reverse their performances from year to year, or even weekly, from their previous bests to their worst. No one escapes failure or loss; the hallmark of a good runner is the ability to understand the rollercoaster syndrome of performance. Michael Musyoki, top world roadrunner of 1982, reflected upon this concept in an interview with the well-known magazine, *The Runner*. He states that, "You have to be ready for every race. One day you beat somebody and the next week he will beat you." Trite as it may sound—"You win some, you lose some." Perhaps what runners should develop, along with their speed, is a good sense of humor. The ability to laugh and not take yourself too seriously in light of your failures may be the ultimate sign of success.

5. *Failures Motivate:* Thinking about failure during an endurance event can actually function as motivation to excel for some runners. The thought of failure is so devastating that they are driven to greater heights. The key is to control the fear so that you don't become too paralyzed (choke during a big race). Learn to harness it for your benefit. For example, contemplate the embarrassment and depression you may experience with failure. If these feelings are too unpleasant, they may force you to excel. Bill Rodgers, in his Boston victory over Jeff Wells, stated that when he "saw," in his mind, the headlines in the paper that he finished second, he began to push harder. The fear that failure might occur sufficiently motivated him to surge just enough to claim a narrow victory over the fast-closing Wells.

If you find yourself in a similar situation during competition, visualize, momentarily, an unpleasant outcome and get in touch with those feelings. If it helps you to "dig down deep" into your reserves, consider using this fear as a positive strategy for reaching your goal. When I can see in my mind the digital clock reading 2:30:08 at the finish of a marathon, I push that much harder in the last mile because I know how unfulfilling it is to come that close to the 2:20s and fall short.

6. *Reframe and Take the Risk:* There are many ways to view a situation. A glass is either half-full or half-empty. Do you see the donut or do you focus on the hole? Is success simply reaching your goal or are you successful for trying to attain the objective? Because a setback or failure is a possible outcome, there is a *risk* involved. To avoid the risk is to never have a setback; however, you'll never reach your goal either. Wouldn't it be considered a failure if you never tested your abilities? Besides, according to strategies one through five, if you take the *risk* and make adjustments, when setbacks occur you will eventually reach the destination. What is needed is a reframing or redefinition of failure. The following diagram illustrates the point:

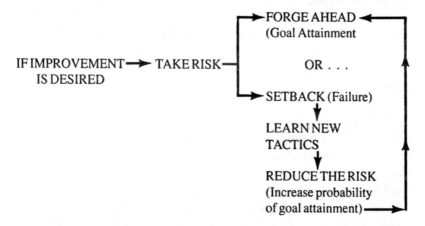

As you can see, improvement requires taking a risk. If you hold back out of *fear of failure* at this point, you *never* attain the goal; this could be considered a *failure*. However, if you take the risk, you will either be instantly successful or, in time, through patience and learning, you will reduce the risk and chances for success will increase. If the goal is realistic (see chapter on Going for the Goal), you will eventually reach the objective. Remember to congratulate yourself for taking those risks; consider it a success. Failure is based on the avoidance of the risk, not the outcome of the event. This reframing process, at the very least, will eliminate those regrets that surface in later years. Risk-taking is quite exciting; you'll never be bored.

7. *Realistic Goals Set the Stage:* For success, that is. Understanding the methodology behind goal-setting is necessary if you want to break the pattern of "failurephobia" (see chapter on Going for the Goal). Setting short, realistic goals increases your chances of success. Practically anything can be accomplished by breaking the task into small manageable segments (if the grandfather clock was capable of knowing how many times it had to tick in its lifetime, it would have quit long ago). The thought of going from a 43-minute to a 36-minute 10K race may seem overwhelming; however, broken into one-minute segments of improvement, your short term goal becomes realistic and attainable. When Alberto Salazar ran his first New York City Marathon, he broke it down into two segments: a 20-miler and a 10K, both of which were quite manageable. When goals are too ambitious, failure then becomes inevitable as all your fears come true. Once again, you are victimized by the self-fulfilling prophecy. The object of this strategy is to lessen the chances of failure by increasing the probability of success.

8. *Self-Focus:* Rather than become concerned about your competition and the outcome of the event, concentrate on your performance moment-by-moment. Dwelling upon the other's talent is a sure way to raise your anxiety which helps to bring about failure. You can't run your best when tense; focusing outward will break concentration. You may begin to channel your energies inward by saying to yourself, "I may not win this race, but I'm in good shape and I'll run quite well. If anyone is going to beat me today, they'll have to run exceptionally well and that's fine." See yourself forcing others to run their best. In the process, you are more likely to be satisfied with the outcome. (See chapter on Alleviate the Pressure.)

The foregoing strategies are productive measures to help you to act in a positive fashion toward failure. It is important, however, to be aware of those times when you might *react rather than act* to the *fear of failure* inappropriately and destructively. For instance, be cautious when you say, "I'm running the race as a workout." Conveniently excusing the performance prior to its occurrence indicates that fear may be present. You need to be honest with yourself in this case. Are you just trying to reduce the pressure to succeed or is it truly a workout? Then there is the runner who, fearing an impending poor performance, drinks enormous amounts of beer the night preceding a race and blames the lackluster exhibition on "being out 'till the cows come home." It is necessary to recognize such self-defeating behavior if you ever intend to "put it on the line," take risks and experience success.

One final word about "failurephobia." Success does not bring true happiness; why should failure produce complete misery? "Tomorrow's another day." Constantly remind yourself of the tremendous physical benefits to be obtained from your running (see chapter on Running on Empty). Becoming tense and stressed over a poor performance negates much of what was gained. Remember when you couldn't run 3 miles? You've come a long way. Not only are a few failures an inaccurate indication of your abilities or potential, they may very well be the key to your success.

FEAR OF SUCCESS

It has been said that in 1981, after he beat Borg at Wimbledon and was accepted as Number 1 in the world, John McEnroe suffered terrible problems of adjustment and identity. In the junior ranks, he avoided reaching the top in his age group. When he suddenly rose to the top in the world, he found it more a burden than a tremendous accomplishment. His game became quite erratic. In his own words, "I couldn't handle it well, and I don't know why." Such is the plight of many a runner who either realizes this beforehand and avoids the limelight or achieves success only to realize the pressures, pain and constant fear of failure that escort the prize of success. Needless to say, John McEnroe has since adjusted to his deserved ranking, yet so many of us continue to undermine our abilities with an unconscious need to not succeed.

The *fear of success* is no hocus-pocus, psycho mumbo-jumbo phenomenon created by psychologists to pad their wallets. The concept was first introduced years ago by Dr. Sigmund Freud who noticed that people have a pattern of becoming ill just when they're about to attain success or just after a goal is realized. "Ill" in this case could actually mean to engage in self-defeating activities as well as, literally, sick. Freud, in his articulate essay, "Those Wrecked by Success," wrote that some people have difficulty enduring the bliss of fulfillment. Regardless of how the fear is manifested, the unconscious sabotaging efforts of such phobics preclude the optimizing of their innate talents and skills.

"Success has ruined many a man," wrote Ben Franklin; and, may I add, many a woman as well. There are numerous negative factors associated with achievement in sport. Exhilarating as it may be, success is frequently accompanied by the burdensome responsibility of living up to one's new triumph; falling short of that accomplishment is viewed as failure. Such pressure alone forces many runners to turn their backs on victory only to be always a bridesmaid, never a bride. Success becomes an albatross, a frightening bird whose "feather in your cap" is to be avoided at all costs.

But don't avoid success—you deserve it all. What you should be avoiding is the fear of success which, at times, can be quite subtle and difficult to detect. Intellectually, we all want to succeed and would verbally deny any thought to the contrary. To best foil the efforts of success-phobia, you must become aware of its subtle common and recurring causes. Insight into its irrational negative aspects is the best antidote for such fear. The following will help to facilitate this insight:

1. *Fear of Self-Knowledge:* Most of us, at one time or another, resist knowing our potential. If you were to *know* that you were quite good at something, you would feel compelled to act or else feel guilty about not developing that potential. And maybe you would rather not act; after all, developing this aspect of self may require hard work, and living up (in your mind and others') to that standard. Becoming totally committed to excellence in running often means time away from your job, your family and your friends. It's a decision that could have painful repercussions. As a result, you may choose a road that avoids success with all its pressures; success becomes a frightening entity. However, if you turn your back on your talent, there is another pain to contend with; you must grow old constantly wondering how good you could have been. Many regrets as a result of not acting in

the formative years could prove to be an even greater burden than the difficulties attached to becoming successful. The choice is yours. Being cognizant of this may make it easier to determine what is more important. If you think you'll have regrets, "go for it" while you are still capable. If not, there's no reason to get down on yourself for calling a halt before success. Being good at something is certainly no reason for doing it.

2. *Fear of Unacceptance:* The need to be accepted by all of your friends and acquaintances could develop within you a fear of success. Subtle pressure exerted by these associates could force you to maintain the conventional status-quo lifestyle. This pressure has been experienced, particularly by women. Gayle Barron, 1978 women's winner of the Boston Marathon, shed some light on this during one of my seminars. She related how difficult it was for her in the infant stages of the running boom because she was a woman "doing a man's thing." Many people still believed during the early 1970s that women should be at home with their families; in running circles, they were considered second-class citizens as they were once prevented from entering the Boston Marathon. It was difficult for Gayle to find support for her avocation. Many women were probably threatened by her running as it forced them to look inward and evaluate their lives.

During the early 1970s, Dr. Martina Horner's studies showed how women were conditioned *not* to succeed. Extra pressure and tension were experienced by women who tried to break away from the traditional stereotypical roles. Things are not that much different today because, although some of society's attitudes have changed over the last 15 years, women still struggle internally with the double bind. They feel guilty for achieving beyond their female friends and feel like failures if they don't.

The bottom line is to understand that if you are successful, some people will have some resentment. To feel twinges of anxiety and discomfort is quite normal; however, if you let it stand in the way of optimizing your potential, you've got a problem. Perhaps the best advice has been given by author-philosopher Mark Twain, "Keep away from people who try to belittle your ambitions. Small people do that, but the really great make you feel that you, too, can become great."

Another form of unacceptance was experienced by a runner who had been ostracized from his "friends" social activities. At the age of 48, he had become a daily reminder of what life could be like if they exercised and this threatened them enormously. Rather than accept his changes, they simply excluded him from parties. They obviously were motivated by the fear that he had outgrown them, and perhaps feared that they would be judged as inferior physical specimens. Many people, when confronted with this reality, would opt for acceptance and back off their goals for success and change. This runner decided to follow his "star" rather than turning his back on self-improvement. To help him confront his situation, I suggested that he communicate his feelings directly with those exerting the pressure. Such a dialogue could evolve in this way: "I sense some changes in our relationship—I feel ignored. My decision to change my lifestyle doesn't change my good feelings for you." Continue your journey toward success; those who truly love and respect you will stand by your side. What better way to test the quality of relationships.

3. *Fear of Disaster:* Very often athletes will shy away from success because they erroneously associate it with the law of averages. If they succeed often, doom or disaster must not be far away. Anything too positive must be countered with danger. The epitome of such illogic was exhibited by a well-known track coach from a major university when he said to myself and the entire coaching staff, "Things have been going fantastically. We're off to a great start—the best in years. Be very careful because this is when something crazy usually happens . . . keep your eyes open for something that may go wrong." Sure enough, they found it. Something did go wrong. This negative attitude was transmitted to the entire team and, as he had predicted, it was "too good to be true." Since the coaches really didn't believe they deserved success (or taken another way, they deserved to have something go wrong because they were *too* fortunate), neither did the team. None of the talent lived up to their potential that year (they easily could have won the NCAA Championship).

Too often I see athletes who are convinced that they do not deserve to be successful. If life is good and they get their way, the message that comes through is "when is this going to end?" I want to unequivocally state that success doesn't necessarily have to result in disaster. You worked hard and *deserve* the best—always. Not thinking that you do will cause you to look for impending doom (negative images once again) and the unfortunate thing about that is that it may, indeed, be found.

4. *Fear of Parental Demands:* Avoidance of success can often be attributed to the subtle or overt pressures communicated to us by parents during our childhood sporting experiences. Parental demands for excellence in sport can force a child to become resentful toward success. Thinking about becoming successful could conjure up negative images of all those early experiences of trying to please everyone but yourself. Success can be something to avoid. I was working with a young national junior champion athlete whose parents claimed not to be exerting pressure on her to excel. Yet that was clearly their perception, as the daughter related how she felt tremendous subtle pressure to succeed. Such "parental pushing" resulted in a drastic decline in her performance, as she consistently placed second to those she beat handily the previous year. She reacted to the pressure by consciously defeating herself. She rejected the chance to be number one at the gate of success. According to this athlete, "Being a success is not worth the aggravation I experience to keep improving. If I fail repeatedly, eventually they'll leave me alone."

5. *Fear of Label "Macho":* Another reason why some of us may shy away from success is the erroneous assumption that to succeed is to be macho, and macho is unacceptable in many social circles. You may find youself hesitating to pass a friend with 50 yards to go in a race because of this. You will certainly fear success and may back off rather than suffer what you perceive to be social rejection. To help with this, a distinction should be made between being assertive and being aggressive. The latter connotes a sense of hostility; winning at the expense of the competition. This is truly *macho*. Assertiveness is the ability to exert influence, make your presence felt, run well and win. It is the pushing of self beyond what you thought was possible. Friends and other competitors are used to help bring out your best. In this sense, assertiveness is positive; aggressiveness is self-defeating, as you use enormous amounts of energy to "bury the opposition." (See chapter on Deflating Competitive Pressure.)

6. *Fear of Failure:* Finally, an overconcern about failure will inhibit your willingness to succeed. Athletes who fear success subliminally fear the erosion of that lofty position once attained. Some runners who have had a few good races will avoid the chance to become the best out of fear of losing and finding out the truth—they would rather live in self-delusion convinced of star status rather than to risk slipping to number two position. The real stars, however, accept the reality of failure and "go for the gusto." Today's victory can reverse itself next week. If you have the ability, your ship will come in if you race frequently. (Reread strategies in the section on Fear of Failure.)

Remember—many athletes *think* they want to succeed. If you haven't yet created success in your life, perhaps a part of you doesn't want it at this moment. You may not feel deserving; you may fear the chances or the possibility of failure that accompanies success. If you really, really want success, you can have it, provided it is realistic. If you feel the slightest twinge or doubt, then it's not for you right now. A clear "Yes" to the question, "Do I really want it?" will bring forth your best efforts. Create in your mind a clear, precise picture of what you want, affirm it, and see it as yours. Keep in mind that it is important in life to have what you want because that will contribute to a state of happiness for you and your supporters.

To avoid risking success or failure is certainly safe from an emotional point of view. However, I reach out to each of you to create the excitement that risk-taking involves and experience a full, wide life. You will not always do your best but, in time, your realistic goals will be reached. Be sure not to measure your self-worth by the outcomes. Release yourself from others' approval; establish your own guidelines for success and strive for excellence, not perfection. Most of all, don't take yourself too seriously. Laugh and enjoy. In the words of Robert Frost, run "the road not taken which will make all the difference." Awareness of the aforementioned success-phobic reactions will make that road considerably smoother.

At this point, celebrate your first success since reading this chapter; that is, success of overcoming these fears that so often impede your running performance.

8

I know of no single factor that more greatly affects our ability to perform than the image we have of ourselves.

... the most dramatic changes that take place ... occur when you abandon a concept of self which had previously limited your performance. My job is to let go of the concepts and limiting images which prevent me from perceiving and expressing my greatest potential.

**Timothy Gallwey
(author of *Inner Game
of Tennis*)**

What You See
Is What You Get:
Self-Image and Performance

Of all the essential ingredients in the recipe for optimal performance in running, it is a positive, realistic self-image that is most crucial. Of course, consistent good training and a huge plate of pasta couldn't hurt the situation. Your self-image is the foundation, the cornerstone, for the pyramid of success (see P.O.P. Chart—Pyramid of Optimal Performance Chart, below). If an accurate, positive self-image is firmly established, the goals on the road to optimal performance will be realized. The reason is clear: once an accurate profile has blossomed, you will tend to choose goals that will be realistic and attainable. They will be in concert with that

PYRAMID OPTIMAL PERFORMANCE (P.O.P. CHART)

profile. The attainment of goals spells success which creates a subsequent increase in the level of your self-confidence. An augmented level of confidence broadens the changes for further success which, in turn, opens the door to optimal performance.

Establishing an inflated portrait can create havoc. It allows for the setting of unrealistic goals leading to constant frustration due to their unattainability. Measuring your self-worth on the basis of *not* achieving these unattainable goals creates a negative image of self which affects future performance. On the other "foot," a deflated image could cause you to severely underestimate your abilities which would impede progress toward improvement. In either case, success in achieving goals is unlikely. In the absence of success, levels of confidence diminish; a lack of self-confidence adversely affects self-image, the vital basis of success. There is, then, in a sense, an ascending order of needs leading to the goal of optimal performance as a runner; a realistic image of self is the key to making this goal possible.

To fully appreciate the effect of self-image on performance, think back to the discussion in Chapter 3 on Visual Imagery and its impact upon the central nervous sytem (CNS). Since images (in this case, self-image) are potent suggestions to the CNS, you will tend to create results consistent with those images 90 percent of the time. Consider the following flow chart:

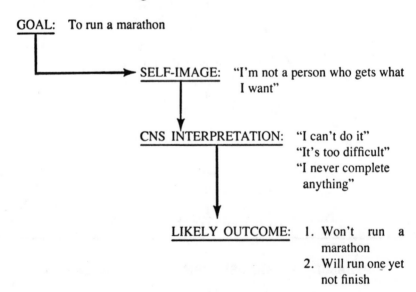

GOAL: To run a marathon

SELF-IMAGE: "I'm not a person who gets what I want"

CNS INTERPRETATION: "I can't do it"
"It's too difficult"
"I never complete anything"

LIKELY OUTCOME: 1. Won't run a marathon
2. Will run one yet not finish

With this in mind, how would you interpret the following story and answer the question posed to me by a runner attending one of my seminars on optimal performance?

> I was never really athletic. In my younger days, the neighborhood kids would never pick me for their team. At the age of 34 I took up running to get into shape and shed some pounds—now I'm hooked on a sport for the first time ever. I've been training diligently for two years and I still can't get below 43 minutes for a 10K race. I'd love to run faster but I guess I can't. I'm a bit clumsy and awkward . . . I can't help it. I've always been that way. Really—I don't see myself as a runner; I don't know why. Have I reached my potential?

In my estimation, Chris has not reached his potential but has created imaginary limits which become "real" barriers because he "sees" it that way; because he believes his images, he will unlikely effect what needs to be done to bring about an improvement in his

performance. Like Chris, each of us carries around a mental blueprint of self. It is based on a rigid belief system formed from our past experiences. Subjective perception of others helps to form this image as well. Once the image is formed, it seems to become the "truth"; its validity is rarely questioned—"Hey, that's the way I am" is an often heard expression from many of us. If our self-depictions are negative, as in the case of Chris, they become preconceived, mythological roadblocks on the trail to optimal performance in running. Many elite and recreational runners appear to be uninformed as to the power of their self-image and the effect it has on their abilities and performance. The reason for this lack of knowledge is not that the subject matter is too complex to understand; they just are unaware of its importance and therefore overlook its value. Yet it is so vital to success in your running that to overlook its effects is tantamount to consistently falling below your potential.

The truth of the matter is that the psychology of self is straightforward and not difficult to understand. Isn't it strange that what most of us seem to know the last about is our own selves; and you spend so much time with this person. Let's take a closer look into this universally ignored aspect of performance.

Most of us operate under the myth that the concept of self is a deep-rooted, unchangeable label to be carried upon our shoulders for life. Although this may be true of many dogs, cats and birds, there could be nothing further from the truth when we are referring to ourselves. You do not act according to some natural, predictable set of laws which force you to adhere to self-limiting beliefs. Your self-portraits are nothing more than a conglomeration of learned information which dictates your actions, behaviors and abilities. It reflects the sum total of all your experiences, thoughts and emotions. If this inner opinion is "I'm lousy at running" or "I'm uncoordinated," you will most definitely behave this way. Picture yourself as defeated and victory will be elusive; believe that you will not be able to run a marathon and you never will. Conversely, creating an impression of self as a winner will inevitably bring success. Once a self-portrait becomes part of your *belief system*, your performance will mirror that image.

It all boils down to whether you *believe* or *think* you *can* or *cannot* do something.

This reality came to me so clearly when, as a 15-year-old athlete, a friend exposed me to an inspirational, anonymous poem. It created changes in my life and I believe it will for you. It's called *THINK*.

If you THINK you are beaten, you are,
　If you THINK you dare not, you don't,
If you like to win, but THINK you can't,
　It is almost certain you won't!

If you THINK you'll lose, you've lost
　For out in the world we find,
Success begins with a person's WILL—
　It's all in the state of MIND.

If you THINK you're outclassed, you are,
　You've got to THINK high to rise,
You've got to be sure of yourself before
　You can ever win a prize.

Life's battles don't always go
　To the stronger or faster one,
But sooner or later the one who wins
　Is the one who THINKS he can!

You must think high to rise and believe in yourself. Performance definitely mirrors self-image. In the words of Henry David Thoreau: "What a man thinks of himself . . . determines, or rather indicates his fate." A perfect example of performance mirroring self-image can be understood by observing the following race scenario of a client of mine:

Paula, a local "hot shot" runner, arrives at the race site one hour prior to the start. She looks around and notices two top females from out-of-town. She immediately says to herself, "I guess I'll take third." Already her images are of failure. She begins to warm-up and feels sluggish. She wonders if she'll feel up to the race. Again, the negative self-talk continues as she says, "I feel lousy today." She is making a statement on the performance to come during a short warm-up, rather than wait until she's in the thick of it. (I have often run my best races after a sluggish warm-up.) Thoughts of defeat creep in as she claims, "I can't beat them today." (They may feel worse than she.) The word "can't" is the most powerful limiting factor in our lexicon. If you think you can't, as the poem states, you are probably correct.

The race starts and Paula begins to think that she doesn't deserve to win. (Her times are competitive with all those in the race, although the "out-of-towners" have a national reputation.) "I'm not as good as they" she states. Feeling terrific and in the lead on the first mile, she turns to verify her position, and strangely, begins to slow down, as if on purpose. (She later told me that she felt as though she made a mistake going out too fast and "I shouldn't have been in the lead"—since she put those runners on a pedestal, perhaps she thought that they knew better by going out more slowly.) With all the negative self-evaluation, she continues to sabotage her own efforts only to fulfill her pre-race prophecy.

In effect, Paula was creating an "on the spot self-image" and acted out that role preventing her from experiencing her true potential. This new image actually affected all aspects of her life for the next few days; in school, at work and at home. She just "didn't feel good about myself." "Everything went wrong."

To see the connection between your beliefs about self and the outcome of your performance, compare what you believe with your actual experience. Notice how you rarely go beyond and experience other than what you believe. The reasons for this are as follows:

First, as explained in Chapter 3, the central nervous system cannot distinguish between image and reality. For example, close your eyes and think of a fresh, sour lemon and notice how you begin to salivate simply by imagining this fruit. This is due to the body responding physiologically to the images that it perceives. If you imagine yourself to be awkward, your body will respond as if this were reality. In other words, what you "see" (imagine) and think is what you get.

Second, there is the theory of the *Self-Fulfilling Prophecy*. You may have been led to believe as a child that you were not bright enough to do well in school. Too many of us were told by marginally intelligent, inadequately trained teachers, that we were dumbbells. This negative evaluation was easily accepted at face value due to childhood innocence. As a result, confidence in learning diminished. You ceased your efforts to succeed. With a lack of effort, failure occurred, thus fulfilling the prophecy that you were, indeed, not bright enough to do well. So it is with running; some people are told as children that they are clumsy, uncoordinated and unathletic. Because of this label, they avoid physical activity in order to escape embarrassment. The act of refraining prevents them from becoming more skilled and, thus, the prophecy that they are unathletic is, once again, fulfilled. Of course, be aware that you may have a legitimate reason for not changing—you may simply not want to change, that's all. Change does require work and you may not be ready for it. If this be the case, your awkardness is probably due more to your choice of not wanting to change rather than to some innate bodily characteristic. Understanding this will make it easier for you if and when change becomes important.

The above theories about the psyche are not without both good and bad news. If your images are a reflection of your experiences and if for many of you, negative experiences far outnumber the positive, you are doomed to negative self-profiles which will interfere with running success. The good news, however, is that there is no reason for you to continue lugging around these negative portraits. They can be changed by creating a "new" you: you are never too young or too old to alter your self-image. Most of us are better than we imagine; Soviet sports scientists are now saying that many elite athletes use only 30 to 40 percent of their optimal potential. For most runners, the figure may be in the 10 to 25 percent range. Creating a realistic self-image does not give you the special gifts to perform any better. It does, however, enable you to release and utilize what talents and abilities you already possess. It is the negative images that inhibit your abilities and keep you from performing optimally. You must put an end to underestimating the magnitude of the gifts you have within by attempting to discover the "true" self. Psychologist Abraham Maslow calls this the process of self-actualization whereby you find out who you really are, how you limit yourself, then dissolve those limitations and begin to achieve your potential. Accomplishing this task requires learning how to create changes in your self-limiting beliefs. It's more a function of what you do about how you are than actually how you are. Therefore, it would help to learn strategies and techniques to enable you to "do" something about changing these old, useless beliefs. You may begin by trying some of the following suggestions. I have used them successfully with many runners, facilitating the development and maintenance of realistic, positive self-images. Are you ready for some enjoyable moments? Here we go!

1. In order to create a realistic picture of self, you must be honest with the evaluation of your strengths and weaknesses. Personal sketches must be a reasonable facsimile of the "real" you—no more, no less. You should consider the obvious physical realities of size, shape, height and weight. That's the easy part. Acknowledging your imperfections and accomplishments, assessing the degree to which you have patience, persistence, thoroughness and other similar traits is quite pertinent but not easy to do. Author Maxwell Maltz, M.D., strongly suggests in *Psychocybernetics* that you avoid creating a "fictitious self which is all-powerful, arrogant and unrealistic. Such an image is inappropriate and will prevent you from discovering the real self." This is not to suggest that you should not recognize your greatness if it is real. Muhammud Ali was truly "the greatest" and lived up to his proclamation. If you are a magnificent runner, affirm that to yourself by saying, "I am a magnificent runner." You may feel strange saying this as it sounds conceited and arrogant. I would agree if you thought you were the only magnificent runner. If you recognize your greatness, as well as all those around you, it would produce a powerful effect on the performance of everyone. Of course, you must also be aware that there is a tendency to underrate and short-change yourself. A negative "self-veto" can be a deterrent to the creation of a realistic portrait. Actually, we all need to learn to take a compliment; more on that later. For now, remember: "You are the architect of your destiny." Build a realistic self-image geared for success; why waste time with an image of failure? As your self-image becomes more positive, the degree of excellence created in all aspects of your life will correspondingly rise. Once a realistic approximation to the "real" you has been created, you are ready to maintain this adequate image by imprinting it in your mind. This is easily accomplished through the use of Relaxation Exercises and Visualization Techniques which you read about in Chapters 2 and 3. Set aside a period of 10 to 15 minutes twice each day, in a peaceful, quiet setting (prior to getting up in the morning and just before falling

asleep at night seem to work well). Become as comfortable as possible. Close your eyes and breathe slowly and deeply through the nostrils. As you exhale, feel a wave of warmth flow slowly from the head to the toes. Use your own preferred technique for relaxation. In this state, you are now ready for the exercise in visualization. Remember that the important aspect of this exercise is to create pictures that are vivid and detailed. Use as many senses as possible in the development of these images. "See" yourself acting, feeling and being as you realistically wish to be: confident, poised, graceful, quick, successful. The central nervous system will process these images to be the "new" you. Remember, you can erase any "old tapes" by recording over them with some that are more realistic and accurate. The following exercise is a variation upon a popular theme adapted for runners:

While in a relaxed state, imagine yourself sitting at a beautiful oak wood table upon which is a group of small mixing vessels and a drinking stein. The jars contain all the things you'd like to be. There are such ingredients as self-confidence, patience, form, power, strength, gracefulness, quickness, excellence. Mix the ingredients you desire for yourself into the stein and drink it down. As you are drinking, feel all the ingredients you have put into the glass flowing through your entire body. Feel them being absorbed into your skin and organs and becoming you. When you have finished, stand up and go over to a wall that is one big mirror. As you look at yourself, see and feel yourself becoming the kind of runner you would like to be and realize that you now are that runner. Know that you will perform as you choose and be successful doing so. At this time, go over to the door, go outside and begin to run. "See" yourself running as you would like, gliding lightly over the ground. "Smell" the trees, "feel" the breeze in your face, "hear" the songs of the birds. You have never felt better; you could go on forever because it feels so effortless. Say to yourself as you run—"I will release all of those beliefs that are preventing me from being all that I can be; I will release any beliefs that will stand in the way of optimizing my running potential." Realize that afterward, the drink will still be taking effect within you and all the things that you desire will continue to be a part of you. Return to the house from where you started and recline on a big, soft couch. You are now ready to return to the regular world. Count from 1 to 5; as you count, feel yourself slowly returning to your usual surroundings. At the count of 5, slowly open your eyes, take several deep breaths, feel energized and rested.

You should consider this exercise as a means to develop any aspect of the self with regard to running: race scenarios could be created whereby you "see" yourself performing well; imagine goals being reached while visualizing your daily workouts; picture how it would feel when you achieve the goals, what your body would look like; see yourself as the runner you wish to be and act according to that script.

2. It might help to emphasize a positive quality that you see in something else that would enable you to expand your self-definition. You may actually possess this quality yet only in small amounts and perhaps you have overlooked it. Many psychologists believe that if you perceive a quality in an external being or thing and find an image for it, you must already possess it. The idea is to pretend and act out

as if you were that someone or something. Identify with the "quality" that the external source possesses. For example—running smoothly, efficiently, calmly and confidently are qualities I possess, yet I lose perspective with them from time to time. I rely on my *image* of Jon Sinclair, as I watched him "fly" effortlessly through his workout on the U.S. Olympic Training Center tartan track. Another outstanding international runner, Herb Lindsay, told me while running together in the foothills of Boulder, Colorado, how often he saw the movie, *The Black Stallion*. As he talked, I couldn't help but see how Herb glided up the steep horse trails with fantastic power and grace. The horse *image* was obviously affecting his performance.

If this approach to a clearer self-image appeals to you, the following suggestions adapted from Syer and Connolly's book, *Sporting Body, Sporting Mind*, should help to perfect the process:

- Choose a quality that you would like to develop—example, graceful
- Who or what comes to mind? Example—Jon Sinclair; a river flowing; a gazelle
- Close the eyes, relax and feel your way into the image
- What does it feel like to be Sinclair or a flowing river or a gazelle?
- Complete the sentence, "I feel like . . . ." with "a gazelle" or "Jon Sinclair"
- While relaxed, see yourself performing in a way that expresses the quality
- Perform your workout physically as if you *are* that image; the more you practice this on training runs, the more available it will be during a race
- Change images when they lose their impact; add new qualities as you master the old
- Turn the quality into an affirmation: "I run smooth and well, just like a gazelle" (see chapter on Affirmation).

3. Self-image transformation (positive or negative) can happen during a race as well. Remember Paula's thoughts as she found herself in the lead after the first mile? She felt she didn't deserve to lead and began to slow the pace. When you get nervous over leading a runner you are "not supposed" to beat, try focusing your attention on your form, stride, pace or how you feel overall. Such concentration, according to Gallwey's theory on *Inner Tennis*, will allow you to immerse yourself in the present and forget the possible outcome. Becoming so absorbed will enable you to get what you deserve—to exceed your expected limit. Focus on the product (outcome) and concentration will drift followed by a concomitant rise in anxiety and sub-par performance. Keep it simple. Choose one aspect of the process (the run) and stick with it. I usually focus on a cadence or rhythm as my pace becomes perfectly synchronized. When this fails, I try to "hear" the beat of a favorite tune and keep my stride in touch with that music.

Many times, our negative self-images have been with us for a long time and this technique may not help change things quickly. Focusing on the moment will be helpful, yet you may want to talk with a sports psychologist who may be able to facilitate insight into how that destructive image developed.

4. Another way to help develop positive self-images is to avoid lowering the expectations that others have of you by telling them the negative aspects of your image. For example, the comments, "I haven't run in five days," "I'm running the race for a workout," "I've done no speedwork" and "I'm out of shape" may momentarily reduce the pressure and positively affect performance. However, images being what they are, you will eventually fall victim to the self-fulfilling prophecy. Besides, you don't want others to think you're a liar so you'll tend to live up to your "advertised image." I know an athlete who chronically relieves the pressure in this fashion. He tells me that he seems to race well because of it. I mention how he may run better if he'd give up this approach for six months; he'll never know because he refuses to try.

I suspect that "silence is golden." Let people have their expectations of you without your influence. I believe that if people expect me to run well, I usually perform up to those expectations. The self-fulfilling prophecy works for you in this case. Take their images of you and understand that they have good reason to feel confident in your abilities. They can always readjust those images based on your performance.

5. The use of *positive self-affirmations* is another very powerful technique in helping you to create and maintain changes in self-image. (See chapter on Language of Success.) This is nothing more than the suggestion of positive phrases (silently or voiced) to yourself. When repeated often enough, they become part of your belief system. This concept is not new. Many of your present beliefs about self are the result of years of negative suggestions from various people in your life. (Remember the awful teacher who called you a dumbbell?) The field of advertising is a good example of how your thoughts and actions are influenced by suggestions. Millions are spent each year to advertise a product on television; political candidates have been elected on the basis of exposure on the tube. Something must be happening. You can, therefore, take conscious control

of those phrases you wish to have influence you. Choose scripts that are brief, positive and to the point. Keep the phrase in the present tense and use rhythmic patterns if possible. The exercise should be performed while in a deep state of relaxation (although not absolutely necessary), with each script repeated and visualized four times. Create personal phrases or memorize any of the following:

— I am a smooth, efficient runner, improving each day

— Every day, in every way, I get better and better

— I am in excellent health and great physical condition

— My mind and body are one; I am in complete harmony

— I am going to set and achieve my goals

— Blue sky, white clouds, feeling good among the crowds

— I am confident, calm and centered; confident, calm and centered

— All of my negative self-images are now dissolved; I appreciate my talents

6. Another important strategy in helping to create changes in self-image is refusing to give yourself subtle "put-down" messages. For example, don't reject compliments. If someone says, "Good race," and your reply is, "I was luckly; I had a good tailwind," you discredit your efforts. A simple, "Thanks, I felt terrific" will reinforce your positive self-image. Making excuses why you look good, or giving credit to others when it belongs to you, fall into the category of "negative image feedback." You may have learned that it is polite to deny a compliment; such "courteous" behavior reinforces the negativism you have about yourself and diminishes the chances of change. Keep reading; you're doing a terrific job.

7. Finally, don't confuse who you are with what you have or have not accomplished. A bad race does not indicate you're a bad runner; nor is it a commentary on your true potential. There's no need to feel miserable if you don't succeed in competition. (See chapter on Failure and Success.) Rather than say, "I'm terrible" or "I can't do it," try to learn the reason behind the "setback" and rest assured that it will not happen again. You are unique; consciously soften up on your own harsh judgments of self; don't you feel like sometimes you are your own worst enemy? Take self-critical opinions with a grain of salt. Refuse to believe them so firmly. Please trust that you

have more talent than you thought. Don't underestimate yourself by using a fraction of what you *now* possess.

When considering changes in your self-portrait to improve your potential, give attention to the words of Reinhold Neibuhr:

> Grant me the serenity to accept the things I cannot change; courage to change the things I can; and the wisdom to know the difference.

Knowing this difference will enable you to minimize your frustrations while maximizing the chances for realistic success. You can definitely change your negative self-portrait. Having the courage to change is the key to that change and susbsequent self-improvement.

9

The mind has great influence over the body, and maladies often have their origins there.

Moliere (French philosopher)

It's All in Your Head: Preventing and Treating Injuries

If the question were asked, "What part of your anatomy is most associated with running injuries?" what could be your response? Do the terms chrondromalacia, Achilles tendonitis, plantar fascitis, myofascitis and shin splints give you a clue? Since the advent of the running boom in the early 1970s, injuries due to musculoskeletal problems and biomechanical imbalance are reaching epidemic proportions; nearly 60 percent of all of us runners will, at some time, sustain an injury serious enough to curtail our addiction. As fanatical neophytes, we get caught up in our enthusiasm, run too much too soon, only to experience sore knees, ankles or feet. Experienced runners increase the mileage base abruptly, resulting in severe injuries, such as stress fractures, acute muscle strain, sciatica and fatigue. Failure to stretch, coupled with improper warmup, increase the chances of injury, as will running surfaces that are hilly, irregular, sloped and banked. Inadequate, unstable, poorly constructed running shoes will also contribute to serious impairment. Technological advances in the shoe industry have been extremely helpful in this regard, yet injuries still abound.

As you can see, the genesis of running injuries is multifaceted, making diagnosis and treatment quite complex. Popular approaches to such remediation tend to concentrate on the physical aspects of the problem itself: we identify the knees, the foot, the muscles and the tendons as the culprits. However, these are simply the anatomical regions where the injury is manifested. Research is convincingly showing that it is the *mind* that is most associated with the *origin* of injuries. It appears as though "it's all in your head." This is made possible as the *mind* is responsible for causing the *stress* which interferes with normal bodily functioning setting the stage for impairment. The *mind* and *body* are interrelated in such a way that many of the

129

respected health professions are now suggesting that proper management of excessive, prolonged stress could lower the incidence of injury in runners. Many more questions than answers are available. However, the increasing discovery of the mind's hidden powers in this regard are numerous, useful and worth considering.

THE MIND-INJURY CONNECTION

To what degree can psychological stress hamper performance by making you more injury prone? And, once injured, to what extent does stress interfere with and delay the healing process? I refer you to the Stress-Injury Flowchart (Figure 1). Recall the effects *images* have on the body from the discussion in Chapter 3. Specific physiological changes occur based upon the images the mind develops. Picturing an event (race) as stressful due to the pressure of winning or achieving a goal will cause responses that will inhibit performance—blood will shift away from extremities (legs and feet), flexor muscles in the legs will contract and the extensors will become inhibited. Such a defensive posture makes the body vulnerable to muscle and tendon problems. In addition, anxiety will interfere with your ability to concentrate; inability to concentrate increases the chances of accidents occurring.

Through appropriate stress reduction techniques, the probability of injury can be greatly lowered. This book's chapters on Fear of Success and Failure, Relaxation, Self-Image and Changing Attitudes for Better Performance, will help you to gain greater control over such stress.

Once injury occurs, you will be subjected to even more stress which will significantly interfere with the healing and recovery process. Being injured is, in and of itself, stressful. Not being able to perform as expected brings a myriad of emotions: withdrawal effects result in depression; anger sets in due to inability to perform optimally; anxiety becomes rampant as you entertain the queries: When will I run again? Is the injury more serious than it appears? How will I get by until I can resume running? Where can help be obtained? How long will this go on? Failure to provide adequate answers to your fears creates a solid foundation of frustration, amplifying each of the foregoing feelings. Such feelings of anxiety, depression and

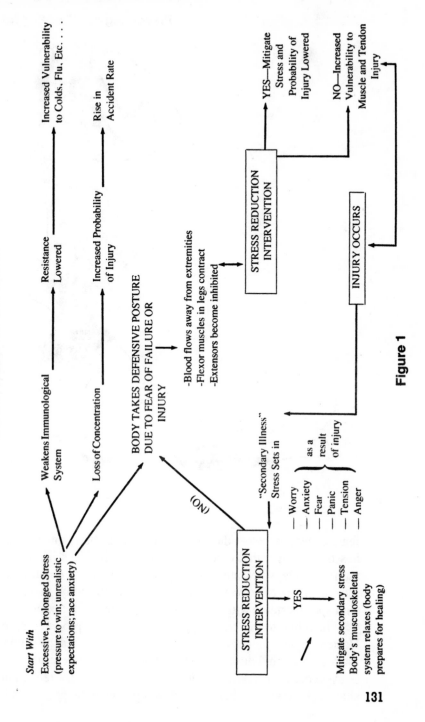

Figure 1

131

fear, known as "Secondary Illness Stress," actually intensify pain. It has been shown that emotional disruption in one's life aggravates pain and delays healing. This happens because the emotional stress reduces the circulation to the injured area of the body, maintains tension and interferes with the elimination of harmful toxins.

Inability to rid the body of these toxins prolongs recovery. Hastening the process of healing is accomplished by mind over matter—the mind directly controls the level of anxiety and stress the body experiences. When emotional stability is restored, pain subsides and recovery is hastened. If you perceive the prognosis for the injury as hopeful, anxiety will diminish. Exactly how this happens is an area largely unexplained by the health professions. However, modern medicine and psychology do acknowledge that the body and mind interact to produce such beneficial results; techniques for facilitating this process will be discussed later in this chapter.

UNDERSTANDING STRESS FOR PERFORMANCE

With respect to athletics, and running in particular, what is psychological stress and how is it manifested? First of all, things or situations are not stressful—it is our view of the circumstances that cause stress, not the circumstances themselves. Running hills increases anxiety for some while others regard them as sheer joy. Hills are hills; they don't change. What changes is how you choose to view them and this will determine how they affect your performance. It is the same for an important race; becoming anxious and frightened by "the wall" in a marathon, for example, may raise the stress level to such a point that it could inhibit muscle fluidity slowing you to a snail's pace. Severe cramping and injury are distinct possibilities.

The psychological repercussions are the same whether stress is perceived as positive or negative. As long as it's *excessive* and *prolonged,* the chances of injury and illness occurring is greater than in the absence of stress. Olympic gold medals can play havoc with their recipients; public interviews, speaking engagements and endorsements are the wonderful rewards to be reaped, yet often are escorted by much anxiety and stress.

You can never eliminate stress—it will always be there. It can be controlled and modulated, however, so that it becomes an asset for super-performance. Hans Selye, an expert on matters of stress, once said that "Stress is the spice of life . . ." For runners, it is the spice that enhances the taste of adrenalin (secreted during times of stress). Anyone who has ever watched Olympic triple jumper, Willie Banks, has noticed his pre-event warmup as he gets "psyched" listening to the tunes on his cassette player. As with most elite athletes, Banks finds that his performance is optimized by raising the level of stress and flow of adrenalin with music. Certain tunes are energizing for you, I am sure. The Rolling Stones put me in perpetual motion. Caution must be taken, however, as you can become over-

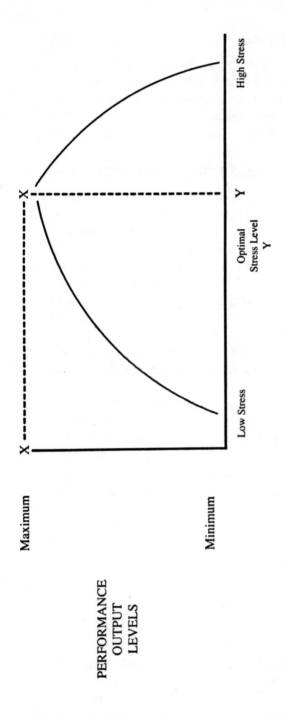

RUNNING RELATED STRESS LEVELS

Increasing level of stress will raise performance level up to the point of optimal stress (Y), where performance will be maximum (X). Beyond this point any additional stress will show diminishing returns for performance.

Figure 2

stimulated. Too much stress and you'll burn out; too little and you'll be "flat." I listened to 45 minutes of rock music prior to a marathon only to be quite drained at the start. On the other hand, I tried a half-hour of yoga followed by a 15K race. It took 5 miles before I realized that being "mellow" and racing are not too compatible. For a graphic portrayal of the relationship between stress and performance, take a look at Figure 2—the Yerkes-Dodson Law of the Invert U.

PHYSIOLOGICAL AND PSYCHOLOGICAL WARNING SIGNS

Before stress can be managed so that it will work for you, it is crucial to become familiar with its warning signs. Stress is sometimes quite subtle and insidious in nature, catching up with you before you know it. By then it has taken its toll. Therefore, the key to successful management is to identify it in the early stages. Althought it's impossible to identify every instance of nonproductive stress, the following will aid in the discovery of physical symptoms:

- Inability to sleep night after night
- Frequent minor accidents
- Constant and frequent colds or flu
- Drastic changes in appetite
- Constipation or diarrhea
- Constant anger
- Nightmares
- High blood pressure
- Low back pain
- Constant fatigue
- Restlessness and uncontrollable "chatter" in the mind

Unlike the physical signs of stress, the psychological indicators are more subtle:

- Difficulty making decisions that would normally be easy
- Excessive daydreaming
- Sudden increase in drug consumption (coffee included—sorry!)
- Excessive worrying, especially over trivia
- Mistrust of friends
- Missing appointments and deadlines

- Forgetting or confusing dates and times
- Feelings of worthlessness
- Brooding over the unattainment of goals
- Sudden reversal of your usual patterns of behavior

If any one or combination thereof persists over a prolonged period, caution is advised. You may be setting yourself up for injury. Aside from these indicators, the probability of illness and injury occurring is intensified if excessive life changes are experienced in a short span of time. You will find it interesting to evaluate your risk of trauma by taking the following Self-Test. If you have been injured or ill more frequently than usual this past year, you probably will score over 200 on this scale.

SELF-EVALUATION: COMPUTING THE RISK OF INJURY

(Calculations based on events of preceding 12 months)

150-900 LIFE CHANGE UNITS—Mild Chance of Sickness or Injury (50%)
200-299 LIFE CHANGE UNITS—Moderate Risk of Sickness or Injury (70%)
300 + LIFE CHANGE UNITS—Very Likely to Encounter Sickness or Injury (90%)

Event	Life Change Units	Event	Life Change Units
Death of a Spouse	100	Change in Work Responsibility	30
Marital Separation	65	Son or Daughter Leaving Home	29
Death of Close Family Member	63	Trouble with In-Laws	29
Personal Injury or Illness	53	Outstanding Personal Achievement	28
Marriage	50	Revision of Personal Habits	24
Loss of Job	47	Trouble with Business Superior	23
Marital Reconciliation	45	Change in Work Hours/Conditions	20
Change in Health of Family Member	44	Change in Residence	20
Pregnancy	40	Change in Schools	20
Sex Difficulties	39	Change in Recreation	19
Gain a New Family Member	39	Change in Social Activities	18
Change in Financial Status	38	Take out a Small Mortgage on Home ($10,000)	17
Death of a Close Friend	37	Change in Sleeping Habits	16
Change to a Different Kind of Work	36	Change in Family Get-Togethers	15
Increase or Decrease in Arguments with Spouse	35	Change in Eating Habits	15
Taking out a Big Mortgage (more than $10,000)	31	Vacation	13
Foreclosure of Mortgage or Loan	30	Minor Violations of the Law	11

The scale shown on the top portion of the test (Self-Evaluation: Computing the Risk of Injury) was developed by Dr. Thomas Holmes and Dr. Richard Rake (the University of Washington School of Medicine) to study the effects of stressful life changes on the health of over 5,000 diverse individuals. The study confirmed the notion that the higher the score, the greater the risk of illness. For our purposes, the higher the score, the greater the stress—and the chances of injury will increase considerably. Use this scale as a predictive measure enabling you to take precautions to reduce the changes or problems arising; also, see it as a tool to help you understand why you have been sick or injured so frequently.

STRATEGIES FOR PREVENTION AND HEALING

Strategies and techniques for the application of the mind in the prevention and treatment of running injuries are numerous. The following are a few of the more popular ones that I have used successfully with athletes:

1.   *View Injury Differently:* As previously discussed, your perceptions of a situation often serve to increase the level of stress experienced. Therefore, alter your perception and the stress level will surely change. For example, why not see this "down time" as a period of rest and recuperation. Take a much needed break and gather the psychological energy you need to be hungry once again for training and racing. Many an athlete has bounced back after being sidelined, with greater determination to achieve higher levels and stay free of injury. World class Japanese marathoner, Toshihiko Seko, is an outspoken believer in the concept of mind over matter. Having been injured for almost two years, he returned to the running scene with a superb 2:08:35 marathon, 22 seconds off the world record. Keep in mind that your view of a situation is a conglomeration of your expectations as well as your perceptions about a situation. The wider the gap between the two, the greater the stress experienced. If perceptions are similar to what was expected, disappointment, as well as stress, will be minimized.

2. *Visualization for Healing and Prevention:* In his book, *Getting Well Again*, Carl Simonton, M.D. demonstrates the incredible success he has had using visualization exercises with cancer

patients. Images are so powerful, he finds, that they can prod the immunological system into destroying the greatest malignancy. His research indicates that a high correlation exists between positive treatment results and positive attitudes of patients using mental imagery in conjunction with other, more traditional therapeutic approaches. Athletes can use visualization in the same way when injured. It works because if all the fears and anxieties of being injured restrict blood circulation to an injured area and delay healing, then the elimination of those destructive emotions through relaxation and visualization will allow normal blood flow to occur and facilitate the healing process. Relaxation allows the body to function normally by decreasing stress; visualization gives powerful messages to the brain to stimulate the flow of blood to the injured area. An effective way to employ visualization is to "see" in your mind a specific healing process taking place: imagine white blood cells entering the area; picture the area getting stronger as you see the muscles repair. Become creative and picture hundreds of tiny people massaging that area; "apply" a powerful ointment and feel it penetrate deeply into the injured muscle. Once the treatment has taken place, concentrate on yourself running as you did before the mishap. Project yourself into the future, completely healed and healthy, with lots of energy to go beyond your previous level of accomplishment. The key to hastening your recovery period is to follow the prescription of your physician, get plenty of rest, eat a good diet and use these mental healing exercises three times per day. Repeat often the affirmation: "Stronger and healthier, every day in every way." Remember that when anxiety and tension are reduced, the pain will also subside. When you stop worrying and let go of the destructive emotions through relaxation and visualization, your blood pressure, respiratory and immunological systems relax and begin to work more effectively in the facilitation of recovery.

Visualization is a wonderful technique for preventing injury as well. This is accomplished through the concept of *ideo-motor processing (ideo* = ideas, *motor* = movement), whereby muscles are activated with ideas, thought and images. This can best be observed when watching a baby move—the infant's small mind *images* what it wants, sends the message to the appropriate muscles and a reaction occurs, however slowly it may be. Movement tends to be jerky and uncertain as the body is processing the message from the mind to the act. As the child gets older, a habit forms and such movement becomes automatic. What we as adults forget is that all our movements originate with an image. I have seen runners hooked up to an electromyograph machine (measures muscle response to thought) and, when asked to visualize running up a hill, the readout indicated that those specific muscles needed for such movement were activated; the athletes were motionless in a reclined position during these tests. With this in mind, to what extent do we create the environment for injury by "worrying" (*worry* = an image of disaster) about how it will happen? If you are *image* twisting an injury may result. *All action is a result of images.* However, you may not be conscious of such images or action—the message travels too quickly (like electrical currents) to be perceived. In addition to the muscles following the thoughts, those images of "potential doom" will cause *fear* and *anxiety* which will contribute to the muscles tightening; such a defensive posture will change your stride and also contribute to the onset of injury. To counteract this, allow the mind, in a relaxed state, to create positive pictures thereby activating the muscles in a constructive, beneficial fashion. Visualize yourself running effortlessly and injury-free. Repeat the affirmation over and over each day: "Every day, in every way, I get stronger, faster and healthier." Such a phrase will allow for a workout free of nervously tensed muscles; worry images will be eliminated. As a result, your body will become less injury prone. While on the run, imagine yourself striding smoothly. Negative injury images may creep in; don't force them away—simply return to your positive posture messages.

The use of *visualization* and *imagery* for the prevention and healing of injuries *(ideo-motor process)* has been successfully used by the national teams of the Soviet Union and other Eastern European countries. Although science is uncertain as to what happens in the mind to accomplish such remarkable results, there are numerous examples in the literature that show, unequivocally, the capabilities of the mind in maintaining and restoring health to the body. I have employed this technology with many athletes who report that injuries that were once chronic are no longer a burden. There's a good chance it will work for you in conjunction with other therapies and precautions. Be patient and give it your best shot.

3. *Laughter Is the Best Medicine:* My grandmother was right. After all these years, her advice has been globally applied with favorable results. She may have been another great philosopher like Kant, who believed that laughter produced a "feeling of health through the furtherance of the vital bodily processes." Sigmund Freud also found humor to be a useful way of mitigating illness. In his book, *Anatomy*

of an Illness, Norman Cousins addresses the healing power of laughter. While hospitalized with a terminal illness, he watched such comedy as Laurel and Hardy, Abbott and Costello and the Three Stooges, accompanied by megadoses of Vitamin C. Ten minutes of solid belly laughter would give him two hours of pain-free sleep. When in complete remission and his health restored, he continued taking large doses of comedy. Research is now showing that not only laughter, but all positive emotions, cause the brain to secrete endorphins which relieve pain and tension. Happiness is one such emotion; like laughter, pleasant, happy thoughts relax the mind and lower stress. Happiness is a habit; if cultivated, it will aid in the prevention and treatment of injuries. The best way to develop such a habit is to begin focusing on the positive aspects of life rather than the negative. When possible, change your view of a distressful situation; there is opportunity in every crisis situation. Being injured may afford you the time needed to complete a special project that's been on hold.

4. *Workouts in the Mind:* Many years ago during civil strife in China, there was an extremely gifted concert pianist who was thrown into solitary confinement for over seven years. Upon his release, he

gave a performance that was judged by a group of experts and peers as having gone far beyond his previous level of expertise. How could this be? Puzzled by this, they asked if he played the piano while incarcerated. His response was that he had put on recitals every day— in his mind, of course. He "saw" himself running his hands over the piano keys, perfectly coordinated and with wonderful clarity. All techniques and form are, to a great extent, dependent on mental coordination. When physical practice is impossible due to injury, illness or even inclement weather, such visualization is invaluable. I strongly encourage you to use this technique of seeing yourself run smoothly, quickly and effortlessly as you were able to do prior to the forced break. Do this in addition to the other strategies while healing; by so doing, the nervous system will enable you to regain your skills faster when you are capable of resuming your training.

Finally, try to talk to others about your feelings. At first, this may be difficult; but when you do, you'll discover that you're not alone. Be assured that, in time, recovery will be certain. Emoting your feelings will also release tension and anxiety. I strongly encourage athletes to maintain contact with training buddies. They will be totally understanding and give you much needed support. In addition, try to keep this time of recovery in perspective; you've had many setbacks in life and overcame those in good form. Concentrate on what you *do* have—a good job, a wonderful family, friends—and devote more time and energy to that part of your world. If one point of your star is unlit, there's no need to consider yourself to be in total darkness. The other four points can still light up the night.

The foregoing suggestions are far from exhaustive. You probably have a few of your own that would work for many of us. From my experience, the regulation of stress is crucial to the prevention and treatment of injuries in athletes. The fact that researchers cannot defend the theoretical constructs of such a psycho-physiological connection should not preclude action. Enough evidence suggests that stress and bodily malfunctions are closely aligned. Since stress is a product of how the mind views a situation, we cannot afford to disregard the use of it, along with other therapies, on the road to optimum running health and wellness.

If you are particularly intrigued by this subject, the following books will be helpful:

1. Ardell, D. B., *High Level Wellness*, Rodale Press, 1977.
2. Benson, H., *The Relaxation Response*, Avon, 1975.
3. Lecker, S., *The Natural Way to Stress Control*, Grosset & Dunlap, 1978.
4. Maltz, M., *Psychocybernetics*, Prentice-Hall, 1960.
5. Pelletier, K., *Mind Healer, Mind as Slayer*, Delacorte, 1977.
6. Selye, H., *Stress Without Distress*, Signet, 1974.
7. Simonton, C., *Getting Well Again*, J. P. Starcher.

10

For when that one Great Scorer comes to write against your name, he marks—not that you won or lost—but how you played the game.

**Grantland Rice
(sports journalist)**

Deflating Competitive Pressure: An Innovative Approach Toward Racing, Winning and the Opposition

There is nothing inherently good or bad about winning or losing. It is our view and interpretations of any particular outcome that give it meaning. Growing up in a competitive society, our views, attitudes and beliefs about victory and defeat are learned phenomena taught to us by the media, coaches and other environmental influences. The message has been clear: winning is good; losing is not.

You do not need to be a psychologist to know that if something is repeated often enough, the mind begins to accept it as if it were true. Most of us have been aware for some time that "America loves a winner." Do they not love a loser? The television blares out "the thrill of victory, the agony of defeat"; after years of watching Wide World of Sports on the tube, I, too, began to believe that losing is agony. *Pressure, pressure* and more *pressure* is what most of us feel when involved in a competitive situation. No one ever talks about the silver or bronze medalist. The contracts and endorsements are reserved for the *gold*. The pressure to win is epidemic, touching all aspects of our development—social, emotional, professional, financial, as well as all arenas of performance. It's not honorable just to try or to take part. You must win! And at all costs. We go to great lengths to avoid what we have learned to be *unacceptable*—that nasty word, *defeat*.

Not only do we have the pressure to perform well, there is the pressure to avoid the *"agony"* that accompanies defeat. Being let down, frustrated or embarrassed after a losing effort, are agonizing feelings directly related to our "winning neuroses." To rise to the unrealistic expectations of having to win, placed on us by society, we resort to "beating" others through questionable ethical and moral pathways. The opportunity for gaining social and financial rewards

147

and opportunities through winning "the gold" has driven many an athlete to cheating and drugs. The pressure is real because if you don't produce as an athlete, you'll be dropped by the organization; as a coach, your job will be tentative, at best. Pressure, pressure and more pressure.

I recently recall where a coach at a major university resigned after admitting to administering illegal drugs to a runner in order to improve his performance. The athlete died after the race. Unfortunately, this is not uncommon. Coaches and trainers often tamper with the athlete's vulnerable body; some try injecting pain-killers to keep their star in the games. Of course, it's for the benefit of the organization; anything for a win.

Remember how important it was for Rosy Ruiz to win? Cheating in the marathon has become widespread (or maybe we're just more aware of it) since her aborted "victory" attempt at the Boston Marathon. In a recent California marathon, at least seven runners were disqualified from participating in TAC events for one year. They were caught crossing the finish line although they hadn't completed the full distance. Course monitors astutely detected them turning around short of the half-way mark.

The 1983 Pan American Games had their share of illegalities as athletes were thought to have taken anabolic steroids in order to develop a winning edge.

The latest in scandals has involved the 1984 U.S. Olympic cycling team where some of its members, in order to improve their performances, became involved with "blood-doping." This is a process of reinjecting the athlete's own blood back into the body to increase the number of oxygen-producing red blood cells, thus increasing endurance.

The stories go on and on; the "win at any cost" attitude needs to be re-evaluated and innovative ways of perceiving competition must be devised. We need to do this even if these violations of the rules were to cease altogether because the greatest drawback of the "pressure to win syndrome" is the devastating effect it has on each athlete's *performance*. Our chances for optimal performance are inversely proportional to the amount of pressure we experience. (A distinction must be made between pressure and arousal: pressure is counter-productive, unnecessary stress; arousal, although at times it can be counter-productive, is a necessary stress component enabling adrenalin to activate the body.) For example, I had the opportunity to talk with four 1980 Olympic track hopefuls on their way to compete in the trials at Eugene, Oregon. They had run so well during the previous two years that expectations rose to a crescendo; anything short of two team berths would have been terribly disappointing. As it turned out, no one came close. There were probably many factors involved in their frustrating performance. I won't pretend to understand why no one made it; however, I can say, unequivocally, from being in their company almost daily that the pressure to win a place on the team was enormous. I sensed a wonderful release of tension in the aftermath. I will always feel they deserved a parade for their fantastic performances throughout the year and qualifying for the trials; somehow, I don't feel they received their just accolades.

The elite do not have a monopoly on feeling pressure. I see it constantly at local races. Age-group competition can be like a school of sharks—vicious. I remember a 41-year-old local competitor not registering for a race because his nemesis arrived and was in excellent shape as well. He ran it for a "workout" because he didn't feel up to par. I happen to know he felt pressure to win and defend his title as course record-holder. He never forgave himself because he eventually got to the finish line first, yet couldn't cross it without a number.

There is another local standout who will drop out of contention in the longer races if he happens to be passed by certain contemporaries. The pain of losing for this runner is so great that he'll go to any extremes not to face it, including a DNF.

There is a growing momentum in this country, in spite of these attitudes and behaviors, toward developing approaches to competition that relieve unnecessary pressure. Parent education programs and clinics for coaches of children are showing that winning is not all that it is cracked up to be. They are learning to teach these kids the values of participation and how to enjoy the process of sport. A crucial aspect to these programs is the understanding that much can be gained from losing. (See chapter on Fear of Failure.) Former all-American and professional basketball star, Bill Bradley, once said that "The taste of defeat has a sickness of experience all its own."

John Wooden, former coach of the UCLA Bruins basketball dynasty, knows something about winning. His teams dominated the collegiate ranks for over 15 years. From this perspective, his words have particular meaning: "I don't know whether always winning is good. It breeds envy and distrust in others and overconfidence and a lack of appreciation to those who enjoy it."

In his career, retired coach of Marquette University, Al McGuire, had his share of victories as well. Sometime after his team won the NCAA championship, he was asked what his feelings were on winning. With his quick-witted New York sense of humor, he replied "Winning is overemphasized. The only time it is really important is in surgery and war."

Respected athletes and coaches are beginning to re-evaluate our traditional attitudes, behavior and beliefs toward winning and competition. The incentive clearly seems to be that such changes can affect the athlete's ability to reduce the pressure and enhance performance levels. Let's talk about changes.

HOW CHANGES AFFECT PERFORMANCE

Attitudes, beliefs and behaviors (ABBs) are habits that have been learned over the years; therefore, they can be unlearned and replaced by other, more productive habits. How this can be done will be discussed later in this chapter. For now, it is helpful to understand that traditional attitudes toward racing, winning and the opposition can create a number of emotions which may not act in your favor (fear, frustration, anxiety and tension). When these feelings persist out of control, you experience a subsequent pressure to succeed or to avoid the agony of defeat. Whichever it is, the pressure creates a roadblock to performance; it becomes a limiting factor on the road to excellence. It does this by diverting much of your energy, physical and emotional, to factors unrelated to optimal performance. Such pressure creates tension in the muscles, interfering with the natural fluidity. Emotionally, that same pressure forces you to expend mental energy by just maintaining those destructive attitudes. Changes in these attitudes, beliefs and behaviors will relieve the pressure and create the environment for improved performance.

CHANGEABLE ATTITUDES, BELIEFS AND BEHAVIORS (ABBs)

Before you begin to consider any change in attitudes, beliefs or behaviors, keep in mind that the goal of this book is to facilitate and enhance the pursuit and attainment of excellence; you don't want to change that. What needs to be examined is the process of how you do the pursuing. I observe many athletes reaching perfection only to fall short of that goal and insist upon measuring their athlete's self-worth by the outcome. Perfection is the cul de sac of performance. As a perfectionist, you will always be disappointed by the outcome; you will dwell on mistakes and become overly self-critical, rather than treat the setback as an opportunity for learning and improving.

Perhaps your pursuit of excellence creates within you an obsession with quantity rather than quality. I see this compulsion in the running community where excellence becomes: "How many miles a week are you hammering?" Personal bests become the gauge of measuring one's ephemeral worth as a runner; course records, number of trophies and medals, victories, number of marathons run, the world's toughest, roughest, challenging ultra—the list is never-ending. You could run a sensational race in terms of fluid motion, effortless gliding and strategic genius, yet your comrades will ignore this effort only to ask "What was your time?" and "Did you win your division?" This obsessive concern about outcome is a learned societal attitude; there are many other cultures throughout the world where grace, fluidity and style are the indicators of success in sports. Why do we become so attached to numbers? If your goal is excellence and improvement, why do we fool ourselves with believing that awards indicate progress? I could win a trophy every week, but not run well; on the other hand, after some of my best performances, I've gone home empty-handed, yet feeling quite thrilled with the outcome. Concentrating on numbers can create behaviors that actually hinder your chances for improvement. There are a number of similar ABBs that potentially hinder performance, regardless of your level of talent. World class elite and local competitive recreational runners are equally affected by non-productive behavior patterns. Have you ever experienced any of the following symptoms? Holding on to them over a long period of time could stand in the way of the breakthrough performance you deserve:

1. Constant struggle for recognition among your running colleagues; this is distracting and inhibits ability to focus energy on the primary task of super-performance.

2. A preoccupation to beat others no matter what it takes; measuring your self-worth as an athlete by the outcome of your performance.

3. Impatience with self-improvement to the point where you become moody and temperamental. Such stress saps energy and creates an unhealthy home environment; your family and friends will no longer be the support system you need.

4. Feeling guilty when resting; the loss of self-respect if you don't run for a few days. Guilt is another one of those useless stress producing emotions.

5. Challenging others during your workouts at all times; competing even during a training run as you purposefully surge on your partners to create an impression and gain their respect. Pulling and pushing is beneficial, but "dropping" causes animosity, tension, and other destructive feelings.

6. Constantly seeking external rewards rather than internal benefits.

7. Being compulsively perfectionistic about your training and racing. Perfection is an unrealistic and impossible goal.

8. Habitually condemning yourself for mistakes and shortcomings while performing. Such negativity will hurt your self-image and you perform according to that self-image 90% of the time.

9. Blaming others or external events for a lackluster performance. Such behavior precludes your accepting responsibility for the setbacks. When one takes responsibility for an outcome, they take charge and gain the control so necessary for change to occur. Otherwise, you are a victim of circumstance and begin to see improvement as beyond your control.

10. Treating running as a thing to overcome, conquer and defeat. Such an attitude requires an enormous use of energy, thus diverting it away from the primary task of optimal performance.

11. Creating tension and anxiety over the expectation to win or do well and being depressed when the outcome is unfavorable. Expectations are the primary source of frustration and disappointment. It's irrational to believe that you can win or do well all of the time.

It's crucial to understand that all of us experience one or more of these characteristics from time to time. It is only when they are frequent and excessive that you should be concerned. There is no need, however, for a personality overhaul. They are behaviors which have been learned; and, therefore, can be unlearned, extinguished—or, simply, replaced. "Easier said than done" you say. Of course, yet if systematically approached, it becomes an enjoyable, manageable experience.

I have found much success using the three-step "Triple-A Procedure" for creating changes in attitudes, beliefs and behaviors:

- *A-wareness*—you need to become aware of those ABBs which are roadblocks to performance. You can't change something unless you know it exists. We have just looked at 11 such ABBs.

- *A-lternatives*—behaviors cannot be extinguished unless there are alternatives to take their place. Step two requires brainstorming your options and choosing the viable alternatives from that group.

- *A-ction*—behavior change actually occurs when you "action plan" the alternatives. The purpose of this step is to choose new, innovative ways to respond to the old non-productive ABBs. These new behaviors are derived from the alternatives and become part of you through affirmation and visualization techniques.

In the following section, I will attempt to apply the "Triple-A Procedure" for the creation of attitude, belief and behavior change toward the *race, winning,* and *the opposition.* I strongly encourage you to go beyond my suggestions and develop your own alternatives and actions for bringing about change in these areas. The important aspect of any desired program for change is the necessity to follow the three steps of the "Triple-A Procedure."

A. The Race

Awareness

Traditionally, runners express an overwhelming concern for the outcome of the event; the end, the finish, the results are the justification for the race. Such a shallow, undimensional view disregards the process of the run in favor of the product. In the words of Alan Watts, "People don't dance to get to the other side of the floor"; and, with racing, there must be more to it than getting to the finish line. The process of the race is a crucible of knowledge quenching the athlete's thirst for learning about competitive stress, recovering from mistakes and confronting pain. The marathon becomes a metaphor of life as you travel rapidly through ecstasy, hurt, fatigue and every feeling in the psychological dictionary.

Alternatives

The finish of the race, regardless of the outcome, cannot begin to scratch the surface of what the process has to offer. Viewing the race as an opportunity to learn about yourself and life, it becomes an ideal arena for personal and athletic growth and excellence. Developing this attitude enables you to develop internal strength by being less controlled by the transitory outcome of the race; there is no finish line with a process event. You can't help but to always win.

Action

To process this alternative, try visualizing yourself, prior to the race, running well and feeling good. Tell yourself—"I may not win the event (I could, though); however, I will run well as an athlete and push others to do their best." Because the race is a microcosm of the big picture of life, it truly is a stage where learning about yourself is possible. In most races, if I can perform at the level I'm physically at, I hope to feel proud to accomplish just that. What others achieve says more about their levels of fitness than my abilities. I like to use the following affirmation to help keep this attitude: "Keep my possible pace in the race and show my face." Showing my face is important; I don't want to avoid others because I did what I could do under the conditions.

B. The Opposition

Awareness

In order to be a good competitor in the traditional sense, you must be a good predator; hunt the prey and destroy, annihilate, drop or bury them. In the movie, *Running Brave*, Olympian Billy Mills slows down at the finish line well ahead of the nearest competitor. His coach furiously yells: "Crush your opponent . . . take him for everything . . . then you own him." Such a "killer instinct" is what you must possess to beat the opposition according to this view. The controversial coach, Vince Lombardi, believed that in order to play football well you needed to have a fire in you and "There is nothing that stokes a fire like *hate*." Paradoxically, such feelings as hate create tension, anxiety and worry which are useless emotions sabotaging your efforts to perform optimally. It channels your energies into "putting the opponent away" rather than allowing you to concentrate on your own performance.

Alternatives

A more productive approach would be one that views the opposition as partners or friends who facilitate your growth and improvement as an athlete. Tim Gallwey, author of *The Inner Game of Tennis*, agrees: ". . . who is it that provides a person with obstacles he needs in order to experience his highest limits? The opponent, of course. Then is your opponent a friend or an enemy? He is a friend to the extent that he does his best to make things difficult for you." At a recent local 15-K race, I gingerly eavesdropped on an enlightening dialogue between the first and second place finishers. "I really wanted you today; I wanted to beat you for some time and I ran the best I could to do it." Cleverly, the runner-up replied, "I'm really happy I can be so instrumental in helping you to run that well." Even though he placed second, he offered his opponent a most challenging situation, helping him to run his best. Efforts by the opposition are opportunities to maximize your potential. You must always remember to thank those who finish close to you in a race. After all, if they decided not to compete, there might not have been a contest; personal sub-par performance is often a reflection of the absence of competition to push you beyond.

Specifically addressing himself to this point is George Leonard, author of *The Ultimate Athlete:* "Every aikidoist faces the problem of finding a good partner who will attack with real intent. The greatest gift he can receive from his partner is the clean, true attack, the blow that, unless blocked or avoided, will strike home with real effect." (The challenge that must be there if one is to learn to become an effective defender.) Leonard continues to talk about the great running back, O. J. Simpson, and his need for competing against opponents who were excellent athletes; only with such competition could he have searched the levels he attained.

Action

To help me remember the importance of the opposition, I remind myself in a deep state of relaxed visualization, that I have never been able to match my performance in a race on a training run and this is directly due to my opponent in competition. I suggest using an affirmation such as "My opponent is very important; because he is here, I will run well." While visualizing, I "see" myself talking to this fierce competitor about how we are partners who will offer each other positive challenging lessons about super-performance; your efforts will allow each of you to respond to the best you have. I image both of us laughing and communicating together as if we were best of friends. I eliminate all fear, mystery and tension over the situation by focusing on his ability to help me run the race of my life.

Very often, our feelings about an opponent are based upon past attitudes, rather than actual reality. Real or not, those attitudes must be examined to see what percentage of them are based on fact; how much are they the result of sheer conjecture? Attitudes about others are often far from reality; it is easier to change those attitudes than to try and alter the opponent. In their book, *Sporting Body, Sporting Mind*, John Syer and Christopher Connolly suggest a worthwhile exercise to help transform your attitudes about the opponent:

> Close your eyes and become deeply relaxed. In your mind's eye, recreate a scene in which you are competing against your opponent. Feel yourself warming up and, as you do, watch your opponent prepare himself. Look for his strengths. Is he self-confident? Strong? Agile? Aggressive? Relaxed? Acknowledge those qualities. And, become aware of how you feel, your uncertainties. What advantage does your opponent have over you? Explore how it is that you feel he makes you lose confidence. Take a deep abdominal breath . . exhale. Begin to compete against your opponent and, as you do, something strange is happening. Through contact, you are beginning to absorb some of his positive qualities. Imagine a rainbow connecting your heads and see each quality as a different color. Focus on one quality at a time (take aggression). Realize that you recognize the quality in your opponent because you actually possess it yourself. Feel the quality filter through the rainbow and flow back to you, filling your body and influencing your performance. Do this for each quality, one at a time. This exercise will allow you to begin reclaiming qualities which you have projected onto your opponent. Through this mental imagery, you will change your response to your opponent by building new, constructive associations. He becomes more human and you become a truer reflection of your real ability.

The power of this exercise is in its ability to create self-awareness about personal qualities and, as a result, develop the self-control so necessary for performing up to your capabilities.

C. Winning

Awareness

The traditional attitude of many athletes and coaches that "Winning isn't everything, it's the only thing" has had consequences for many athletes. Recruiting violations in college athletic programs during the 1960s and 1970s took its toll. The introduction to this chapter talked about how the use of anabolic steroids in the world of track and field in order to "win at all costs" has cast a shadow of gloom over international competition. Traditionalists argue that if winning is unimportant why keep score? In response to this, it must be said that the outcome of any event is important, but not as an end in itself. The significance of "keeping score" lies in measuring one's performance throughout the race. Whether you win or not is determined, not by the "outcome results," but by the "performance results." How did you feel? Did you glide effortlessly? Were you able to surge effectively? By concentrating on the process aspects of performance "winning" is almost assured, or at least, the chances of success greatly enhanced.

Dorcus Susan Butt, a Canadian psychologist, suggests that athletes motivated to win in the traditional sense often develop serious emotional problems. They exhibit signs of anger, weeping, sulking and self-imposed isolation. Defeat is rationalized by attributing it to external forces; ("I just ran it for a workout"); blame is projected on others for the loss ("I was pushed going into the last turn"). Many of these reactions were exhibited by some of our top athletes at the XXIII Olympiad.

Alternatives

As an alternative to such traditional attitudes, Butt suggests that a truly healthy approach to sport is an intrinsic perspective that celebrates the mastery of skills and physical-emotional satisfaction. Performance should also be judged over a period of time rather than on the outcome of a few events. After all, you may even be the first one to cross the finish line yet such an outcome can often be an indication of who stayed home that particular day. In addition, a win may be attributed to another's mistakes or their level or lack of fitness. In these examples, "winning" is an overrated phenomenon

—the luck of the draw; rarely, in such instances, does it measure the quality of performance.

It is becoming clearer to many runners that an obsession with winning is a roadblock to excellence; if victory is not obtained, the excellent *effort* expended will be overlooked. More athletes are believing in the benefits of internal rewards. Money, prizes and fame are transitory commodities; few remember your outstanding achievements and, in time, your memory of the event will fade. For example, in the 1976 Olympics, a splendid performance by an American in the 400-meter hurdles earned him the Silver medal, finishing just behind Edwin Moses. How many of us, other than some track buffs, remember that it was the ex-Penn Stater, Mike Shine? Who won the first New York City Marathon? Had Gary Muhrcke not been a personal friend, I, too, would not have known. He ran a 2:31 +, a time that may not even place him in the top 100 today. Yet winning for Gary is not *where* he finished; it's more *how* he performs and feels during the race that matters. His recent 2:23 at Boston at the age of 43 was perhaps a greater treasure than his New York victory.

Action

Part of the obsession with winning is intricately tied into our fear of losing or failure. "Failure" is such a despicable experience that we try to avoid it at all costs. To help change destructive attitudes and behavior toward winning, consider the suggestions on how to come to terms with failure in the chapter on Fear of Failure. In addition to this, use an affirmation such as "I may or may not win; I will still run like a winner." It's true that it feels good to win and everyone loves a winner; however, putting forth your best effort and enjoying the process is very important.

Another strategy for action would be to visualize, in a deep state of relaxation, your personal definition of what winning is. In other words, winning can be setting realistic goals for the race and "seeing" yourself fulfilling that challenge. Imagine how rewarding it is to take control and define what makes you feel good rather than give to others permission to make you feel inferior or less of an athlete because you fell short of their definition of winning. The point to remember with these exercises on winning is that victory and its rewards are wonderful. Professional athletes, in particular, have a tremendous incentive to win. However, I suggest a change in orientation; by focusing on your realistic challenging goals (or the team's) and seeing the event as a process of playing well throughout, the payoff, the win and the prizes will ultimately be yours. If not, rest assured that the outcome might not even have been that wonderful if you had not used your new mental approach.

Finally, understand that winning is not always in your best interests. I have worked with many "successful winners" who felt that the victory was the best thing ever to happen only to admit, in retrospect, that it wasn't as good as they had imagined it to be. I don't suggest turning your back on a chance for success; just keep those expectations in perspective. Above all, if by defeating someone, you somehow feel more worthy of respect at his or her expense, you may want to examine your definition of winning and determine its ultimate effect on performance.

Having read these ideas, you may want to decide where to focus your energy. Perhaps there is no need to change anything at this time. Your attitudes may be working for you. However, if you think you'd like to chance a change to test your present beliefs or if there's a sense of something missing from your running, and your progress toward excellence seems stymied, examine the relevance of these concepts for your program of optimal performance. Take a look at your beliefs regarding competitive events, the opposition and winning. Those beliefs could be the limiting factors in your performance and overall health. To help rid yourself of restraining beliefs, become relaxed, go to your place of peace and repeat the following phrase five times: "I am now willing and able to release all those beliefs that are interfering with realizing my optimal potential with running."

A FINAL THOUGHT

Running is a fantastic sport—a gift to enhance your life. In an age when there's so much potential for conflict and chaos, running is an opportunity to compete cooperatively with great respect for the opponent. It is a chance to dwell on internal personal accomplishments, rather than those external failures. Running could become an instrument for personal inner calm whereby you shelve the "killer instinct," an attitude which inevitably permeates all aspects of life.

One of my roles as a Sports Psychologist, is to modulate the enthusiasm of those who win for winning's sake. There's so much more, aside from victory, to be gained from sport: personal and social development, physical and emotional wellness are but a few of the wonderful advantages of competing. Aggressive, assertive participation in running is healthy, but not at the expense of others. Since running tends to be a microcosm of your personal world, how you relate to all your opposition will carry over into the other aspects of life—job, relationships and family. I would predict that for many of us, how the running goes, so goes your entire world.

If your goals with running are to optimize performance, to maintain overall fitness and health, consider changes in attitudes toward the recognition and fame of competition and winning. No amount of fame can bring inner satisfaction and happiness; it is a transitory entity and if accepted as such, could be a wonderful experience. Jim Fixx, in discussing this short-lived nature of fame, stated that, "I could see myself starting to slip back into the obscure life I had led before" as his book began to sink lower on the best-seller lists. In the words of Pierre de Coubertin: "The goal of the Olympic Games is *not* to win but to take part." Harry Edwards, in his *Sociology of Sport*, states that we have so much more to gain as a society if we stress in sport "cooperation rather than antagonism, participation and self-actualization rather than confrontation and domination." And, in the process, we may even deflate competitive pressure and perform beyond our wildest expectations.

11

When all your skills have been
honed to razor sharpness and
when your physical condition is
at its zenith, then the difference
between winning and losing is
generally mental.

Coach Bud Winter
(San Jose State University)

Competitive Psychling:
Your Mental Best on Race Day

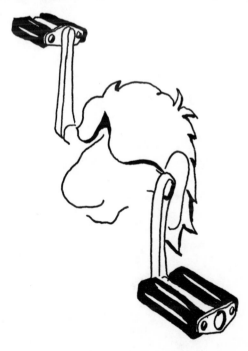

It is safe to say that most competitive runners have a set of guidelines, principles, beliefs or rules by which they create a workable training program. One of the greatest, if not the greatest, milers of all time, Herb Elliott, was no exception. In his words, "My golden rule was to train for the mental toughness and don't train for the physical development." The importance of this statement centers around the word train; to see results from any mental program, you must train each day if noticeable benefits are to be realized. It takes work, time and effort if you wish to develop competitive mental tenacity. The amount of time necessary to see progress, however, is miniscule compared to your physical work-outs. A mere ten minutes each day will provide a cornucopia of new and exciting changes in performance. Although I am not totally sure what Elliott meant by "not training for the physical," it has been my experience that no amount of mental preparation will open the flood gates of performance without your attention to those quality miles. Your goal must be to connect the mind and body in marriage so that they work harmoniously for optimal performance. Assuming good quality workouts, the mind should allow you to perform up to that level of physical development rather than to sabotage the body's efforts to function as it should. In other words, no amount of brain-power will allow you to run a 2:10 marathon, unless you are in 2:10 shape. However, there's lots the mind can do to convince you that you can't do it, even though you are physically ready. The object of "competitive psychling" is to minimize the chances of this happening by training the mind to facilitate, not hinder, performance.

Whereas all of the chapters in this book can help to promote optimal performance, this section will address those specific concerns that most runners have with regard to the competitive event itself. Racing requires particular mental training strategies of its own, given that 90 percent of your performance is based on your mental fitness.

Olympian Benji Durden begins his mental preparation two months before a marathon. According to him, ''Even if I were in the most incredible shape of my life—2:06 shape—I still couldn't run a good marathon if I wasn't mentally prepared.''

What are some of the more popular topics and concerns runners have with respect to race preparation? Questions about levels of arousal, how to raise and lower anxiety, how to maintain concentration during the race, how to remain confident, how to cope mentally with tactical errors (going out too fast, for example) or any other emotionally related problems while racing, as well as concern over fatigue, the opposition, unexpected occurrences (weather changes, crowds, hills) and pain. Some runners even express interest in learning how to cope better with post-race feelings of disappointment, anger or frustration over their failure to perform up to expectations. As you can see, each of these concerns fits into one of three categories: pre-race, during race, and post-race. I will address each category and try to touch upon your mental needs to get you ready for the big day. Although I can't possibly cover each and every concern of each athlete, there will be enough laterality to enable you to improvise and adapt these strategies to your individual needs.

PRE-RACE

When do you start preparing mentally? Some runners, like Olympian Lee Evans, have prepared their minds for years preceding the one big event. Others, like Durden, feel that two to three months will do it. There's no such thing as too soon; the more crucial the race, the earlier you should begin your mental preparation. A rule of thumb is to begin two to four weeks prior to the event. Sometimes I'll train mentally for only two to three days the week of the race, particularly when I'm mentally fit and simply need a ''fine tuning.'' For the purposes of this discussion, I'll simulate a typical program broken into five segments: two weeks, two days, two hours, before competition, during competition and post-race concerns.

A. *Two Weeks Prior*. Your *primary objective* during this segment of mental preparation is to build confidence by drawing from past successes and by rehearsing the upcoming event in its entirety; anticipating the unexpected and reacting favorably to such occurrences is part of this visual imagery rehearsal. Your basic tools for achieving those tasks are *relaxation* and *visualization*. Apply the principles discussed in Chapters 2 and 3 directly to the following suggestions. What follow are guidelines meant to give direction; you should certainly feel free to experiment and create your own scenarios. You are only limited by your imagination.

Although not an absolute must, benefits can be derived from knowing the course in advance. If it's local, drive or bike it in both directions and even run various sections. If not possible, get a description from someone who has run the course; oftentimes, race directors will provide the information upon request. Knowing what lies ahead will build confidence before as well as during a race. Surprises cause anxiety which takes a toll on confidence. Eliminating the unknown is a distinct advantage for optimal performance. I clearly remember running the California Summit Marathon, a brutal course winding up and over the Santa Cruz mountains. The illusion that most runners had after 11 miles of uphill, was that the remaining part of the race was gravy—and they would coast down to the finish. Much to their chagrin, they were greeted by a series of four challenging inclines at mile 22 and, as if to add insult to injury, the finish chute was perched at the top of a 300-yard rising grade. Fortunately, for me, I ran that final 4-mile stretch a half dozen times prior to the race and clearly planned my strategy with those undulations in mind; I "saw" myself gliding up the hills and finishing strong. I was not to be denied that day as I squeaked out a narrow victory ahead of some talented runners who were on unfamiliar ground. The "home court" was an advantage in my favor as I truly learned the meaning of "There's no place like home." If at all possible, use the actual race course when mentally preparing for an event.

Using experience such as this has helped in my preparation for other races to capture those positive feelings of fluidity, effortlessness and strength. In a relaxed state, you want to visualize how you felt during previous successful performances. Get in touch with those memories and transform them to the upcoming event and the course you'll be running on. Recall how quickly and smoothly you ran, how you glided past others, how you surged throughout and floated across the finish line in a personal best. Remember—that was YOU and it can be repeated. I strongly urge you to begin your rehearsal by "seeing" yourself one hour before the race—Is there grass around you? How does it feel, smell? How do you look as you warm up and jog to the starting line? "See" yourself composed, poised and confident, ready to burst forward like a contained horse let loose. As you rehearse the race, get in touch with how it feels to run your best and imagine the race unfolding exactly as you would like it to. Carry your visualization through the award ceremony (if that's in your plan) and into the evening. See yourself enjoying the fact that you performed well earlier in the day; imagine what it would be like eating your favorite meal with close friends discussing the race. Don't leave anything out. Researsal should encompass every aspect of the entire day.

This brings up an important point. How can you rehearse all aspects of the race when the unexpected usually happens? After all, running the Boston Marathon can mean the possibility of being exposed to unpredictable weather conditions. You rehearsed the perfect race except you forgot to do it in the driving wind and rain. Unless you plan to run in San Diego or Phoenix, the probability of climatic changes is a reality to contend with. Also, other changes and unexpected scenarios may conflict with your rehearsal. Perhaps there are many more people in the race than expected or your nemesis decides to show; both situations could ruin your plans. Therefore, it is crucial that you include in your visualization of the event all these extraneous possibilities that come to mind in what is called simulation training. Some situations, obviously, will remain unpredictable. It's impossible to cover all eventualities.

Coach Bill Squires has his runners simulate physically the unknown by having them push and surge when they least expect it. Like physical simulation, the mind needs to be trained to respond favorably in case you're exposed to something not planned for. The key is to think of all the negative possibilities (don't plan on snow or cold if the probability is minimal), include them in a few of your rehearsal sessions and "see" yourself responding to the unexpected in a positive, effective manner. Simulate mistakes made while racing, only to recover from them successfully in the mind as you would like to as if they actually occurred.

Practice, in your relaxed state, overcoming false starts; responding assertively to being passed on the track; feeling confident even though the high jump runway is not to your liking; performing well if the crowd is obnoxious; coming on strong in a race where you have been tripped or any other "unforeseen" circumstances. I wouldn't dwell on these aspects; simply see them as possible and build the confidence needed to respond appropriately. If it's scorching hot, adjust to the heat and "see" yourself running a desired pace for these conditions. You may want to change your strategy and run faster if you're fortunate enough to pick up a tailwind. Planning for its potential will allow you to easily adapt. I have seen many a runner's confidence at Boston shattered as they woke up to freezing rain. This need not happen with simulation training.

Other objectives for mental preparation during this two-week period would be to focus upon your confidence and self-image (see chapter on Self-Image) with the use of affirmations as seeing yourself running your workouts according to plan. Visualization works quite well for training runs; since you race as you train, this is not to be overlooked. Those difficult, grueling speed runs will be met with joyful anticipation if visualized as such. Rehearse the workout just prior to putting on your gear; "feel" yourself surging with the power and grace of a beautiful stallion; "see" the splits on your watch as they indicate how great you are performing. Imagine the nutrients flowing to your muscles; say to yourself, "I feel great, I feel fantastic; better and better." Remember that your muscles will tend to follow the images of the mind. If you imagine the run to be a chore, the body will fulfill that prophecy. You may not have a great workout as a result of pre-planning, but I will predict that it will be better than you originally believed it could be with all those negative images. If nothing else, being in a relaxed state prior to a strenuous run will allow the body to run more fluidly and improve the circulation of the blood with its vital supply of oxygen.

B. *Two Days Prior.* The bulk of the work has been accomplished and there's very little that can be done physically to help your performance. Undoubtedly, you will have tapered your running in the final week, or cut back on training regardless of the event of your choice. Emotionally, there are some vital issues that concern most athletes. Anxiety, tension and loss of concentration are now factors to contend with as you are geared to act, not sit and wait. It becomes exponentially more difficult to focus on the event as mind "chatter" interferes with the imaging process. The more importance placed on the event, the greater the need to control these entities. Your primary objectives during this segment of mental training are two-fold: First, although you are reducing your physical output by tapering, you should increase the frequency of the mental rehearsal you have been doing for the past few weeks. Broaden its scope to include images of the ideal athlete, as well as thinking about your best past perform-ances with their ingredients for success. Get in touch with that "feel-ing" and project it into the upcoming event. Second, you should begin to gain greater control over your external environment (your home, your friends, your activities) so that your internal emotional self can do its job of focusing on the event. Discovering what works best for you is crucial. Some athletes like to be around friends and go about their business as usual. Others find it important to be alone and modulate the otherwise noisy, distractive environment. What-ever you choose, be sure to feel eager yet controlled. It's the point at which, when you give the word, the energy will flow. "Contained enthusiasm" would describe the feeling. If you feel emotionally flat, don't become overly concerned; I will show you ways to arouse your-self quickly prior to the race. Getting anxious over low levels of arousal will actually drain precious energy. Again, environmental modification will help to regulate anxiety and tension and improve concentration, helping you to focus more sharply.

Another technique to help with anxiety and concentration is the proper use of ritual. The more familiar your routine just prior to an event, the more control you have over anxiety; ritual is a habit requir-ing little or no thought and, subsequently, reduces tension and fear over the possiblity of forgetting something at the last minute (dietary, equipment and travel concerns are a few). Aside from this, the ritual becomes a familiar stimulus which serves to remind you of the up-coming event. For example, when I begin to "carbo load" before a marathon, I know the race is three days away; when I climb into my racing shoes, it's now post-time—here comes the adrenalin. Such a training mechanism takes the place of thinking, "The race is about to begin; am I ready?" The simple act of putting on the shoes will stimulate the appropriate emotions. Everything I do in the last 48 hours is part of a ritual. It gives me confidence because it's something familiar—I've been there before. Such behavior explains why some athletes will wear the same singlet or shorts. If they raced well with these garments, you'll never see them in anything else. It's superstitious behavior; but so what, it works. I traditionally "catch" a movie—nothing too heavy or draining—two nights before the race. It diverts attention from the event and helps to improve my sleep. Dinner is also part of my routine. The night before the race, I eat the same food that has worked well in the past. If I'm on the road, I'll take it along in case it's not available. By race morning, there are no surprises or extra trips to the porta-toilet.

Benji Durden has rituals. The next time he's at a race nearby, try to locate him as he huddles in a quiet corner reading a mindless novel. He states that by reading, "I'm forcing my mind to concentrate on something other than the race. I'm trying not to use up any adrenalin before the race."

Another helpful ritual I like is a checklist of all that needs to be done: arrange for travel; set the alarm to wake me up (two if I'm nervous); fill the tank if I'm driving to a race; gather clothing to be worn pre-, during and post-race; pin race number to my singlet; pack Vaseline, water and racing shoes. Not worrying about these items allows me to concentrate on the event itself.

The notion of rituals is universal in sport. I have worked with professional athletes in the NFL (National Football League) and other elite amateurs and, without exception, they all possessed idiosyncratic behaviors for the purposes of being better prepared emotionally. They all agreed that the effect is the elimination of worry which improved the chances for a concentrated, relaxed performance.

The key to making rituals work is consistency. No matter what routine you establish, be sure it's a consistent, bit-by-bit pursuit. By so doing, you will begin to experience a more consistent optimal level of performance. If something that worked for you in the past no longer feels good, junk it. Don't be consistent for consistency sake. Remember that "foolish consistency is the hobglobin of little minds." Always welcome a change in the routine if there's a chance it will help.

C. *Two Hours Prior.* The night before the race and up to two hours prior to the start, call a halt to your visualization exercises. Your brain is a muscle and can use the rest during these hours. Relaxation exercises prior to bedtime, however, will facilitate deep sleep by quieting the mind and regulating the flow of adrenalin. While in a deep state of relaxation, think thoughts of calming scenes, happy times and anything that will slow the chatter in the mind. Avoid any thoughts, if possible, about running. Upon awakening, follow your routine and give attention to any last minute details. Two hours prior to the start, whether in transit or at the race site, begin to focus on the matter at hand—the race. Your primary objective during this final count-down phase is to regulate your level of arousal (or anxiety) for optimal advantage and to rehearse, for the last time, the complete event as you would actually perform.

With regard to arousal level, if it's too low, you'll be flat, unmotivated, and the possibility of mistakes during the event will increase. Too high a level and you will become tight, uncoordinated and terribly anxious, which could increase the chances of injury as well as contribute to early fatigue and loss of concentration. A sub-optimal performance is likely to occur. According to the "inverted-U theory" (see chapter on It's All in Your Head. . .), you need an optimal level of arousal in order to perform maximally and this level will vary for each of us. Two things are certain: the simpler the task to be performed, the greater the amount of arousal that can be tolerated; and, the better prepared you are for that task, the easier it will be to tolerate high levels of arousal. You must determine your needs. For distance racing, you probably want to go to the starting line full of "controlled vigor," ready to burst forward in an effortless start at the sound of the gun.

How much and how little? If your legs are tight, your breathing shallow and irregular, your throat too dry, your hands unnecessarily cold, your concentration scattered or your stomach feels strange, your arousal level is probably too high (levels 4 or 5 below). If your competitive spirit is lost and you feel listless, you may need a shot of adrenalin (levels 1 or 2 below). On a scale of 1 to 5, rate your level of anxiety or arousal prior to a race:

	No Anxiety (Arousal)		*Controlled Vigor*			*Very Anxious (High Arousal)*
One Week Before	1	2	3	4		5
One Day Before	1	2	3	4		5
One Hour Before	1	2	3	4		5

Five and ones a full week before can be tolerated with little or no effect upon performance. The day prior to the race, you should be circling 1 or 2, maybe 3; but certainly not 4 and 5. This is the time to conserve your emotional energy. At one hour before the event, level 3 would be most beneficial; if you're not there, you can and should regulate your emotional energy to that level of "controlled vigor"—a high level of excitement and enthusiasm, coupled with loose, relaxed muscles. Perhaps you already know this feeling. It's highly subjective and, with experience, you will be able to identify the cues that signal "your day." If you keep a log of your workouts and competition, be sure to record those feelings that were present on optimal performance days, then try to recapture them for each competitive event.

How does one manipulate arousal level? Once you determine whether your emotional state is too high or low, you can apply a variety of mental strategies to regulate it to a desirable level. The following techniques have been used by many of my clients and athletic friends quite successfully; the list is not exhaustive, yet I'm sure you will be able to adapt some of them to your mental training program:

WHEN TOO ANXIOUS OR AROUSED. Because anxiety cannot be contiguous with relaxation, the object of these exercises will be the creation of a relaxed environment, internally and externally.

1. *A place of peace:* Choose your favorite mode for relaxation; when the mind is quiet, visualize yourself alone in a place that is peaceful and calm, indoors or outdoors, and where there is no likelihood of being disturbed by others. Perhaps you have been there before or maybe you are creating one in the mind. For me, a mountain resort nestled in the pines on a clear sunny day is perfect. I can "smell" the trees, "feel" the breeze, "taste" the pure mountain water and "see" the birds, clouds and streams. The house is furnished with all the necessities and conveniences. It's a place that's safe and isolated from the confusion and chaos of the race scene. I usually do this exercise away from all the stimulation—someplace under a tree or in my car, alone. From this place, you can rehearse the race, focus on your self-image or simply "see" yourself running smoothly and effortlessly. Create any situation that will facilitate calm and tranquility. Use the place often when

you need to gather your thoughts and be relaxed. What you visualize will vary from race to race, depending upon your needs.

2. *Music exercises:* A wonderful source of relaxation and anxiety reduction is music; either humming a peaceful tune, or listening to one in your car or with headphones will calm the nerves. Classical pieces from Bach or Vivaldi and the music of George Winston help me tremendously when I'm overstimulated.

3. *The black box:* I took this exercise from John Syer and Christopher Connolly's book *Sporting Body, Sporting Mind.* It works quite well when overly distracted and when you need to concentrate on

the race in a relaxed manner. As with exercise number 1, go to your place of peace. In your mind, sit in a big soft chair before a large desk. Pick up a pen and write down on a piece of paper whatever it is that is distracting you. Hear the point of the pen slide over the paper as you write. When you finish, put the pen down, fold up the piece of paper, and place it in the black box on the right side of the desk. Close the lid and turn around facing away from it. Promise yourself that you will attend to it after the race and be sure to do so in the relaxed state. You must trust that part of you that was promised attention later on will get the attention. Now, come out of the relaxed state and attend to the business of the race. Distractions can be anxiety producing and interfere with proper focusing. This exercise is so effective that a gymnast was once able to ignore blisters on her hands by "putting them in the black box." You decide how you want to use your box—it's powerful.

All athletes are different and must develop their own approach. I know of some world class runners that, rather than go "inside" themselves, mill around talking with others only to find out that they're not alone in their anxiety. Some will read to get their minds off the event. Others actually think that it's a tremendous benefit to be anxious and, if they think that way, it will be of help. Prayer plays a big role for some; by putting the race in the hands of their God, they feel less pressure about the outcome and this results in lowered anxiety. Whatever your choice, if it works, you'll perform well.

WHEN TOO CALM OR UNAROUSED. The purpose of these exercises will be to help you overcome a flat, uninspired performance by stimulating the flow of adrenalin and creating a positive level of excitement. Some athletes perform while being too relaxed because they interpret this as being "ready"; however, being too calm and lethargic has as many drawbacks as being at the other end of the arousal continuum. The following exercises will help the body to get revved; if you still feel "blah" and unenthused, consider not racing that day and run it as a workout:

1. *Breath control:* Clench your fists, tighten your jaw and begin to take short, rapid, deep breaths. After 60 seconds, you will notice the body's tempo quickly elevating. Take more time if needed. Be careful not to hyperventilate.

2. *Rapid focus:* The object of this exercise is to stimulate the incoming of information to the brain. Focus on an object, person or place; quickly observe every possible detail. Rapidly change your attention to something else and repeat the process. Your eyes and head should scan the environment as quickly as possible, focusing as you go.

3. *Music manipulation:* Just as you used music to create calm and tranquility, choose favorite tunes that energize. It's difficult to remain "mellow" with "up" music. Carry a walkman cassette or blast the sound from the car tape deck. Come alive with the sound of music by manipulating the tempo and volume.

4. *Prance or dance:* Any form of rapid movement to include quick, sharp turns and fast steps will affect your energy level in a positive way. Three quick steps forward, turn left for seven rapid strides, turn right and briskly walk—keep it going for a few minutes. Dancing to the music will also assist the flow of adrenalin and elevate your heart rate.

These exercises are not mutually exclusive. They blend well and create a more powerful effect when used together. Experiment to see what works best for you.

D. *During the Event.* The moment has arrived. It is time to put it all together; you have planned the work, now work the plan. In an ideal situation, the event will require little mental energy other than steady concentration and your body will react instinctively to the demands placed upon it. This rarely happens however. More than likely, you will be asked to respond to a myriad of emotionally charged circumstances that will test the outer boundaries of your mental stamina. Distractions, as well as negative thoughts, filter into your cognitive structure sending distress signals to the body. Fear of slowing to a snail's pace, being passed by other competitors or possibly not finishing the race create unwanted anxiety and tension. Then, of course, there are the elements of fatigue and pain, old friends that would love to come along for the ride. Some situations will be entirely familiar; you may even have planned for them. Others will be totally unexpected. In any event, your work will be cut out for you. The following represent the more recurrent areas of concern that athletes have brought to my attention and strategies to help ameliorate them:

1. *Distractions:* Sometimes pain is a positive distraction; it could be your body's way of signaling distress and deserves your attention. If you determine that it's not serious, then the distraction should be "shelved." For example, the onset of a "stitch" can be an internal distraction, but its effect will be minimized if you concentrate on the rhythm of your breathing or the cadence of your stride. Perhaps your distraction is external; you wish the race were over and you're worried about a work-related problem. Try using the "black box" technique previously discussed. Remember that any distraction will persist if you resist. Rather than expending energy fighting the distraction, view it as a friend who "visits" occasionally. Give it credence by talking to it: "Hi, it's you again; well, I'm busy right now so how about talking later." This will give you greater control over any anxiety that may arise from having the distraction. Also, see it as a challenge or an opportunity to practice concentration while on the run.

2. *Fears:* Many runners' mental breaking point is tested when the outcome of the race looks dismal: fears of slowing, not finishing or being passed in the late stages are demoralizing. The brain sends messages to "throw in the towel" with phrases such as "Let them go, it's not important"; "I'd rather be at that picnic; who needs this" or, "It's too much farther to continue." Whether you are an elite or recreational athlete, the fears and anxieties are similar. The first step to help deal with this crisis is to focus on what can be done now. Don't think about the future (the rest of the race, tomorrow or the day after). If the grandfather clock knew how

many times it had to tick in its lifetime, it would have given up long ago. Divide the task into small, manageable segments. As that runner goes by, he looks exceptionally fresh and he's running quite faster than you—hang on—not until the end of the race (or at least tell yourself that)— but for 1 mile or 6 minutes—or whatever is comfortable. At that segment, re-evaluate your feelings. At the very worst, you will have run better for that distance than if you had given up. At best, you may catch a "second wind" and run one of your best races. By telling yourself that you only need to follow that runner for a short distance, the task doesn't seem as psychologically overwhelming. And, above all, those runners are probably as tired as you but want to look " convincing" as they go by. When they see you stick like glue to their side, they may begin to slow down and this will be a confidence building situation for you,

3. *Refrain and reframe:* Thoughts during a race play an important role in performance. Research has shown that the body's use of oxygen improves when the athlete's mind focuses on positive thoughts. Changes in your emotional state can be experienced when you change your thoughts; behavior and performance follow your psychological makeup. When negative thoughts infiltrate your emotional space during a race, simply acknowledge their presence and immediately substitute a positive self-affirmation. (See chapter 13.) Negative thinking is normal; everyone has it. Because the thoughts are there is no reason to believe they will materialize. Choose only those thoughts that will work for you. The body will follow only those messages that the mind transmits. You are in control. As you approach a gruesome hill, refrain from seeing it as an unexpected barrier. Reframe and say to yourself: "Hills are friends that develop my conditioning. They are opportunities to give my body a rest from the pounding."

4. *Uncomfortable Exertion:* It usually happens in those races where you elect to push for a better performance. It can indicate that you are running a good race, but it also hurts—you feel the pain of exertion. Remember that you are not alone; everyone feels just as bad or worse. The feeling is usually amplified if you're racing alone so try to hook up to a small group and tuck in behind. Concentrate on their strides. Also, I find it psychologically more helpful, particularly in the last few miles of a marathon, to tell myself that I can handle it for 16 more minutes rather than to think in

terms of 3 long miles. Remind yourself, before you decide to let up, that you may have regrets after the race for not pushing. The discomfort you feel now may be nothing when compared to the pain of living with yourself following an unsatisfactory performance.

E. *Post-Race Concerns.* A complete program for mental race preparation should consider the athlete's feelings and concerns following the event as well as those prior to and during. Management of post-event tensions, anxieties, frustrations and disappointments is vital because of their potential negative effects on future competitive efforts. Time out should be taken to examine the meaning of a win or loss; put into proper perspective, there is much to be gained from such analysis. For example, you may not have come in first yet your performance was a personal best; besides, you may have learned some valuable strategies for future competition as a result of not coming in first. Interpretation of the outcome as a success or failure should be cautiously handled. A loss is not necessarily an unsuccessful effort. The chapter on Fear of Failure and Success should help you to better understand and interpret your performance for future competition. From my experience, most successful runners will wait until the day after their event to more objectively criticize and assess the outcome. I want to stress the importance of taking ''alone time'' to rehash your thoughts; do this on a slow, gentle run, or take 15 minutes and relax—go to your place of peace and ask yourself: ''What have I learned from this experience that will help me to develop my potential?'' In a relaxed, calm state, you will be able to analyze the situation more clearly. Some runners find it helpful to record their findings in their race log; at the end of the year, they possess a lot of valuable, useful guidelines for better performance.

In addition to this, the relaxed state can be used to visualize the negative aspects of the performance and what you now feel you might have done differently to change the outcome. Go through the entire race scenario again, this time changing the story to the new script.

Practice this successful version often before your next event. By so doing, you will change all the negative associations you have with this performance and increase the chances of the new script happening when faced with a similar situation.

Performance on any level requires an athlete to deal with the psychological as well as the physical. To overlook this "whole" is to leave the outcome to luck or chance. Such uncertainty is unnecessary; you can gain greater control over the task at hand (or foot) by experimenting with the various mental strategies and techniques just discussed. To wish yourself luck is to admit to being out of control. You will begin to take charge of your performance and optimize the chances of success when you race with your head as well as your body. Sharpen your mental game plan and begin to enjoy the benefits a trained mind can bring to your sport.

12

As the ravenous leopard needs to stealthily focus on its prey in order to feast, the athlete, hungry for excellence, must totally concentrate on the task at hand if success is to be devoured.

**H. Cheng
(Chinese philosopher
—runner)**

Concentration:
Reconnecting the Mind
to the Task

It was during the 1976 Olympic games in Montreal, that the world watched, embraced and "adopted" the sweet and charming 14-year-old Rumanian gymnast, Nadia Cominici. She captured our hearts so easily with her unremitting determination to win the gold, which she did successfully with a series of perfect "10s." Yet the machine-like quality of her performance, coupled with an emotionless expression of the face, led many viewers to believe that she had had her "child" stripped from her being. Certainly this couldn't be a normal adolescent; what had they done to her? When the truth was known, we learned how Nadia cried with exuberant joy following her outstanding performance. Her "child" was set free; what we had seen as she approached each event was the epitome of intense, deep concentration, a learned skill taught to her by Rumania's optimal performance specialists. She was in a relaxed state of complete alertness to the task at the exclusion of distracting environmental factors; she was aware of nothing other than her routine.

Many coaches and trainers of athletes seem to agree that the most necessary psychological factor for optimal performance is absolute concentration. Whether or not this is true is open to discussion, yet one thing is for certain; without the ability to focus completely, your true potential will probably never be realized.

An outstanding American athlete who relates well to this statement is high-jumper Dwight Stones. After watching him perform for the last eight years, he gets my vote as Mr. Focus. As legions of viewers in the L.A. Coliseum waited for his moment in the sun during the XXIII Olympiad, the media cameras were able to capture his intense concentration prior to each jump and signal it into the homes of millions throughout the world. Dwight seemed completely oblivious to all this attention, going about the task as if he were alone in a home gymnasium.

Why are such powers of concentration so remarkable? After all, babies easily seem to be able to focus intently on an item of interest without distraction. Observe a one-year-old as it ponders a toy sailboat floating in a tub. Noise or sound of any kind won't take away the purposeful attention given to that boat. Have you tried calling to a child who is involved with an activity? Forget it! The reason young children can focus so well is because they do not feel as though they are being evaluated. As adults, we quickly become aware that our performances are judged. Such evaluation causes our attention to be diverted. Competition is an arena of evaulation: scores, times, heights and distances; all measurements of how you are performing. This means people are watching and this interferes with the ability to focus. We become self-conscious and this divides our attention between the audience and the task. It becomes exponentially more challenging to perform up to our ability. When the mind becomes disconnected from the task, for whatever reason, the task becomes more difficult.

I recently worked with a talented high school runner who was experiencing this disconnection. She came to me ostensibly for mental strategies to help her regain her successful form from the previous year. She had been the league champ, undefeated in every meet before her senior year. After a lengthy discussion, it became quite clear that parental pressure to win and secure a college scholarship was the primary concern, not mental strategies. Social and financial restrictions were punishments handed down to her by her zealous parents in order to "help" her improve. Paradoxically, they forced her into a rebellious mode; she unconsciously began to sabotage her own efforts. Her mind was filled with "chatter" and concentration was lost. It was the parents who needed help in understanding the dynamics of the situation. Once they did understand, they eventually backed off, and her ability to focus was recaptured. She began to excel, once again, as her mind became connected to the task rather than to the external parental pressure.

From what you have just read, it becomes clear that concentration is the learned skill of being alert to the task while simultaneously excluding unimportant environmental factors and internal distraction. In addition to having direction (internal or external stimuli), concentration also has width. When Robert Nideffer talks about width of attention in his book, *The Inner Athlete,* he means the ability to select a narrow or broad focus. Width is like a tv camera that can focus on the entire lead pack in a marathon or zoom into the lead runner's face a split second later. Like the camera, the skill of concentration requires an athlete to manipulate focus in order to choose the proper direction and width necessary for that task. For example, the high jumper would tend to select a narrow, internal mode of attention. On the other hand, in the early stages of a marathon, an astute athlete may focus back and forth from narrow to broad, from internal to external. Internal factors include fears, expectations, fatigue and doubt; external factors might be weather conditions, course terrain, lighting and the ubiquitous crowd. The objective of concentration is to focus on what is important while minimizing the distraction. The following procedures will help you to develop ways of enhancing and controlling the objective.

ATTENTION-GETTING PROCEDURES

The use of specific procedures to recapture your diverted attention before, during and after an event is highly recommended. The only alternative is to leave it to chance; that is, you may or may not be able to regain your focus for the remainder of the competition. Not being able to do so could result in consistent sub-par performance.

The following procedures have been proven to work with athletes of all abilities. Recall the times when you tend to become distracted and choose the most appropriate procedure for those situations:

1. *Give Credence to the Distraction*
    The distraction does exist so don't deny it; if you resist, it will persist. Putting enormous energy into fighting it will only increase its intensity. For example, fatigue is a universal distractor that causes most distance runners to panic, tighten up and become even more fatigued. It creates a fear—the fear of pain or of not finishing—which, in turn, causes stress and tension that interfere with muscle fluidity. A strategy that seems to help is to give credence to it—yes, it's there; then try talking to it as if it were a familiar friend coming along for a run. For example, "Hi fatigue—it's you again. You always seem to visit me at this stage of the race. That's fine—you can come along if you wish, but I'm going

finish. So speed it up and join me if you'd like." By conducting such a conversation, you automatically reduce the anxiety by refusing to fight and expend energy over this extraneous nuisance. It can be readily applied during the actual event, or prior to it as you visually rehearse by simulation (see Chapter 3, Visualization).

2. *Become Stronger in Your Attraction to the Object Focused Upon*
   Whatever it is that you wish to concentrate upon, create a way to become more attracted to it. For example, to focus more clearly on your stride, concentrate on cadence or rhythmical beat. A baseball player concentrating on hitting the ball could focus on its red stitching or the printing on the leather. Runners concentrating on form can often watch their shadow on the road when the sun cooperates. Imagine your lungs expanding or heart pumping when concentrating on breathing or blood flow.

3. *Internal Distraction—Focus Externally*
   When irrational fears or doubt or fatigue creep into your thoughts, begin to focus externally upon the closest runner's feet and look for the stitching on the shoe. Or, if you're sitting around waiting for an event to take place, relax and go to your "place of peace" (see chapter 3, Visualization) to gain control over your environment; open your eyes while still relaxed and focus on a simple object like a stone or a blade of grass. Absorb its details—color, shape, texture. Imagine yourself so small that you could hide behind the object. The purpose of this exercise is to focus your attention toward external factors; this will take your mind away from the internal distraction by forcing attention to the outside.

4. *External Distraction—Focus Internally*
   When weather conditions, crowd noise, rough terrain and other external distractions hinder your concentration, go into a relaxed state and visualize your event as necessary components of a good performance. If externally distracted while competing, begin to focus on stride, breathing or form. Make your attraction stronger using procedure number 2 above.

5. *Change Interpretation of Distraction*
   Remember that it is your view or interpretaiton of the distraction that makes it so. Rain may be an external distraction for many, yet those who run well in those conditions do not see it as a problem. When I teach an athlete deep relaxation, I mention that any noise heard during this state will only contribute to a deeper calm.

From that moment, they interpret any sound as a facilitator to relaxation rather than a distraction. You could do the same for distracting rain; the flowing drops could be "coating" you with energy. I love the feeling I get from running intensely up hills. Because of that, hills in a race are a welcome sight—I enjoy them yet my opponents become anguished; for them it's an unwanted distraction. As you saw with the first procedure, reinterpreting fatigue as a friend gives you greater control and makes it less of a distraction. In order for this procedure to work, you must practice the reinterpretation prior to the event by anticipating possible distractions and changing your view of them. It is best done through a relaxation-visualization sequence. If you can't change the distraction, change your view of it and it will cease to be a distraction.

PRACTICE EXERCISES IN CONCENTRATION

Once you have the procedures that work for you, the next step is to train the mind to focus more easily. The following exercises will help you to practice and gain greater control over your ability to concentrate. Even if you have some of your own that work well, you may want to give some of these a chance as they have worked well for other athletes. Expand your repertoire of concentration skills by selecting those that work best for you. Remember to follow all the guidelines for relaxation and visualization if used before the event. When such distractions occur during an event, your previous practice will allow you to simply use replacement thoughts without the relaxation and visualization.

- *The "Psychic Goretex Dome"*

    Think for a minute about the miracle running gear made with Goretex. Acting like a semi-permeable membrane, it allows the small molecules of body moisture to escape while keeping out those larger particles of snow and rain. For the purposes of this exercise, I ask you to become relaxed and in the "mind's eye," see yourself covered with a "Goretex dome." Like the hostile elements of weather, the distracting stimuli are still there; you can still recognize them, yet the "dome" selectively keeps them from penetrating. You do not respond to them emotionally. Visualize them trying to reach you only to be rejected by this "psychic wall";

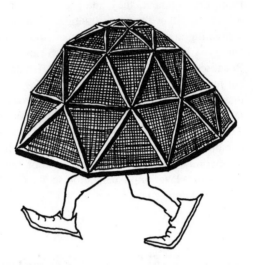

see yourself viewing all the distractions and smiling because they just can't harm you. In a sense, you stay "emotionally dry."

● *The "Stop Sign of the Mind"*

Have you ever noticed that signs, simply by their shape, cause people to react. The octagonal stop sign, painted red, seems to help drivers depress the car's brakes. The object of this exercise is to apply this logic to distracting thoughts which break concentration prior to or during an event: fear, anger, frustration, anxiety and hate are but a few. In a relaxed state, bring into focus a situation which conjures up such distracting thoughts; for example, the fear of being passed in the last mile of a marathon, or the fear of your hand catching the bar during a high jump. As you visualize this thought creeping into your mind, interrupt it by "seeing" a stop sign and simultaneously yelling, in your mind, the word "stop"; I usually ask an athlete to actually yell this word prior to the exercise so that he or she can easily recall how it sounds. Immediately after the shout, replace the thought with a constructive phrase such as "I will run well and keep my position" or "I will jump clear over the bar with room to spare." Change these statements when their power begins to fade. Also, as you practice this visualization, gradually begin to lower the intensity of the shout from an all-out scream to a gentle whisper. Practiced often enough, it will work for you on the spot, prior to or during an event. I have used this in the later stages of a marathon when my mind becomes distracted with ''I want to stop, this is awful.'' I reply with —stop—and, then, ''I will finish feeling better and better; I get stronger and stronger.'' As you will see in Chapter 13 on Language and Success, the mind will follow your words. Be aware that some thoughts may be too difficult to extinguish. Perhaps you need the ''Goretex dome'' or simply treat it as a real entity and tell it you'll deal with it later. Also, you may not find the stop technique works. I sometimes use nail-pinching—pressing fingernails into my palms until it hurts—then say the substitution phrases. The techniques, if practiced often enough, will work well—give them time. Remember to rechannel your thoughts immediately, from the split second those distractions set in.

● *Candle Gaze*

This technique works quite well the evening prior to an important event when your mind is racing out of control. Go to a quiet room, sit in a comfortable position, and stare at a lit candle noticing the contours of the flame, its colors, and changing shape. Close your eyes after five minutes and recreate every detail in your mind. Do this back and forth until you are able to focus on how good you feel—''Calm and confident, I will run well. Today is my day.''

● *The Isolation Camera*

This exercise works well just prior to an event when you wish to keep your head together when everyone else is losing theirs. It is a process of selectively narrowing your attention from the wide world of sports to one specific aspect of your own performance. In a deep state of relaxation, begin to visualize the following:

a) Think of a large circle. Within this circle, ''see'' many sports being played simultaneously in different segments of this area. Focus on each one individually and then scan the space until you hit on another. Make believe you are a camera.

b) When you get to the track-and-field and distance runners section, ''see'' in your mind all of the activity going on; someone is pole vaulting, others are sprinting and still others are on the road running a 10K event; focus your camera within that circle.

c) After a few minutes, focus on your event. Draw a circle around those participating and, as you watch, begin to see yourself emerge.

d) Draw a circle around only you and continue to see yourself as if a tv camera were isolating its focus on you. Watch yourself perform well.

e) Begin to focus on part of your body and narrow your concentration to that area. Draw a circle around that part of you and notice everything down to the slightest detail. Stay with this picture for a few minutes.

f) Focus the camera on your feet and, in particular, your running shoes. Notice every slight detail of those shoes as you use the slow motion capability of your camera. "See" the impact of the shoe as the sole compresses against the road surface. Concentrate totally on your smooth, efficient stride and rhythmical cadence.

● *The Fruit Bowl*

In a relaxed state, visualize a bowl of your favorite mixed fruit. Imagine yourself shrinking in size, small enough to climb into the bowl. Climb around on each piece of fruit and "feel" the texture. Now become so small that you are able to climb inside a chosen

fruit. How does that feel? "Smell" the aromatic fragrance and "taste" its flavor by taking a big bite. Look to the outside world from inside that fruit—how does it appear? What color do you "see"? As you climb out of the fruit, notice how the juices have covered your body. When you do, gaze at the bowl of fruit and see if there are any changes. Notice the piece of fruit that you discovered from the inside.

- *Fantasy Projection*

This exercise works well when your present environment is somewhat chaotic and confusing. This could be prior to or during your event. I remember standing in the gymnasium waiting for my number prior to the 1977 Boston Marathon. In those years, 2,000 runners was a huge turnout; I thought I'd never make it to the starting line. I determined that this was irrational and plenty of time remained before the noon commencement. In order to better focus on my purpose for being there, I became deeply relaxed and visualized the peaceful calm setting of a beach in Panama, one that I had visited many times. Because of my familiarity with that environment, I was able to imagine with explicit detail scenes of the white sand and turquoise water, the blazing sun and the crystal blue sky. I actually projected myself back in time to a period of restful tranquility. While at that beach, I rehearsed in my mind the race strategy I planned to use and "saw" the outcome of the event unfolding in a most favorable way. It is best to choose a place where you have been, one that evokes clear, positive images. This will facilitate your ability to focus on that particular spot as well as concentrating on the upcoming performance.

- *Focus Breathing*

This strategy is particularly helpful if your inability to focus is brought about by unnecessary, unpredictable stress. Use the same technique from Chapter 2 called "Deep Abdominal Breathing." However, when you inhale, visualize the air carrying molecules of concentration into your body. As you exhale, "see" all that stress being blown out the nostrils and floating far away. The incoming air is like a tranquilizer that furnishes the calm you need to focus on the event.

- *Diversion Thinking*

Quite often, athletes become preoccupied with that useless, superstitious behavior—worry. The result of such a demon is heightened tension and a loss of concentration. This exercise will help to extinguish the flame of worrisome activity before an event and particularly during the thick of competition. When worry sets in, shift your attention automatically to your feet—how do they feel? Then switch to your buttocks. Focus on how it feels. Give attention to your jaw and face muscles. Are you relaxed? Tune into your arms and feel their synchronous movement. Now back to the feet—then the stride—then your buttocks—then your face—back to your arms. Tell yourself that all's well; no need to worry. Begin to focus on your game plan once again.

● *Slow the Flow*

In a quiet, peaceful place, close your eyes and relax. Imagine an hourglass on a table in front of you. As you "sit" at this table, let your mind slow the flow of each grain of sand as it filters through the opening, one grain at a time. Slow it down until it takes about 15 seconds for each of the individual grains to move from the top to their new location. Observe each one's texture and "see" how they jockey for position to enter the opening.

● *Explore the Distraction*

You're running the first mile of a distance event and become distracted because you don't feel too good; your breathing is off, and there is a general feeling of malaise. "Oh no!" you say, and begin to lose concentration. When in the middle of such negative experiences, allow yourself to explore those feelings; try to focus on what they can teach you. Manipulate your pace, stride and form for a few minutes to see the reaction. Being open to these distractions will enable you to experience the normal cycles of competition; once you feel all right about this situation, the distraction will ease up and your ability to focus will improve. If you happen to be tremendously rundown or have a bit of the flu, perhaps the decision to run should be re-evaluated.

● *Mantra Chanting*

Many Eastern cultures have developed their skills of concentration by rhythmic breathing to chanted mantras. A mantra is a word or phrase repeated vocally or subvocally. The syllable "om" is an example of one you may recognize. Atheletes involved with Transcendental Meditation (TM) have found their mantras to be quite helpful to their ability to focus. You can experiment with any phrase; try making it rhythmical to coincide with your stride. For example, "Run strong, run long"—one word per step.

As you can see, exercises in concentration are quite diverse. They seem rather simple, yet the results are powerful. From what you have read, you should now believe that you can take control of all those annoying and distracting situations, whether they be internal or external. The key to success is to remember that concentration is a conscious vigil; an athlete need not leave it to chance. Following these guidelines and exercises is no guarantee that you'll perform better on any given day. There are too many variables to make such promises. Also, no technique or strategy can assure 100% attention to a given task. You can usually expect a certain amount of mind drifting. Hopefully, by feeling in control and using some of these suggestions, you will be able to become more thoroughly involved in your experiences—much more than you had before you gave it this much attention.

13

Words create reality. Keep them positive and they will provide the power to transform the quality of your existence.

an old Irish proverb

Affirmations and Quotations: The Language of Super-Performance

I am the greatest, I am the greatest!

Without a doubt, these are the most famous words ever spoken by an athlete in our time. Sports enthusiasts throughout the world know him by the name Muhammud Ali, perhaps the greatest prize fighter ever to step into the ring. Love him or hate him, you must admit that he walked, talked and fought like a champion. In his words, "I dance like a butterfly, sting like a bee." Many spectators were initially turned off to his seemingly braggart style; after all, America loves a winner but loves them to be humble. That he wasn't! Yet his words were an accurate reflection of his talent. He truly was the greatest and simply affirmed that over and over. Affirmations are dynamic phrases that have tremendous power over our minds and, subsequently, our performance. When Ali would say, "I am the greatest," his mind would create an image of success and his central nervous system would process that image as if it were real. Our actions are a reflection of our images 90 percent of the time; our images are the result of words or thoughts. Because of this, words can and do create performance. Of course, what you affirm and image must be somewhat close to reality if this construct is to work. I could chant Ali's words, jump into the ring, shake hands with the opponent and be carried away on my back. Yet running is quite different. Since we tend to underestimate our abilities, repeating positive phrases that go beyond how well we run would be realistic and enable us to fulfill these thoughts. You are the programmer; what you put into the brain (computer) will be obeyed by the body.

WHAT ARE AFFIRMATIONS?

Affirmations are very important components of visualization, so much so that I felt they deserved a chapter of their own. They are strong, positive statements about something that is already true or has the realistic potential for being so. To affirm is to make what is so *firm*. Unlike the endless negative and positive "chatter" filtering into your mind each moment of the day, affirmations are conscious, pre-planned, positive thoughts that direct our actions and behaviors in a productive way. Without them, you leave to chance the possibility of desirable behavior occurring. They are attempts to change patterns of negative thought that, like tape recordings, continue to play the same old counterproductive tune. They enable you to replace stale, worn-out dialogues with new, positive phrases to help develop your full potential. Words can truly transform the quality of your existence.

APPLICABILITY OF AFFIRMATIONS

Like any technique for visualization, affirmations are applicable for practically all situations in life where optimizing the outcome is the primary goal. For example, the creation of a more positive self-image is greatly enhanced through the use of affirmations. During times when you are particularly self-critical, consciously choose loving, caring phrases to help you change the negativity. Tell yourself: "I am talented, intelligent and creative" or "I deserve the best" or "I am abundant and have a lot to offer."

Perhaps you want to create real changes in your physical appearance. "Seeing" yourself as you desire will facilitate your movement toward that dream. Say to yourself: "Slim and thin I run to win."

Use affirmations if you wish to be more self-accepting, to feel good, to develop relationships, to become more creative or even to relieve boredom. In sports, they are quite useful in turning fear into confidence, increasing concentration, preventing you from pushing too hard, becoming less frustrated, reducing self-criticism, sharpening your skills, coping with fatigue, treating injuries and any other performance tasks that you may need to address.

HOW TO CREATE THEM

There are some important rules that you must know about in order to formulate a workable, powerful affirmation. Once you learn these, creating your own phrases becomes a simple process.

1.   Short and specific. Make the affirmation a clear statement of your feelings. If they become too wordy, you tend to get lost in the verbiage.

2.   Rhyme and rhythm. Developing statements that have a cadence and rhyme tend to become more deeply impressed into your cognitive structure. For example, "Better each day, in every way."

3.   Present tense. Avoid using the future tense because the mind is literal and will always see it "as if" it were still coming. For example, instead of "Thin and trim I will run to win," say "Thin and trim I run to win." Don't be concerned that it hasn't happened yet. Act as if it has.

4.   Positive posture. Using words like "won't" or "don't" may be picked up by the brain unintentionally. Avoid saying "I no longer push too hard"; replace it with "I pace myself well." Affirm what you want rather than what you don't want.

5.   Expect success. When you formulate a phrase, suspend disbelief and doubt for the time being. Just go with the thought.

6.   Affirmations are best used during a deep state of relaxation and should be repeated 10 to 20 times on every attempt.

7.   Index cards. Create your affirmations and write them on individual index cards to be displayed where you can see them daily: on a mirror, refrigerator door or by your night light.

Once you know these rules, you are ready to apply them to the construction of your personal affirmations. I suggest that you follow one of the following two guidelines:

*   CHANGE NEGATIVE TO POSITIVE: Quite often, your mind will give you a negative statement that you accept as fact: "My opponent is better that I" or "I'll never improve" or "I always tighten up in the important marathons." Create affirmations by changing these to the positive: "I run as well as my opponent"; "I get better and better"; "I stay loose as a goose in all my marathons." Try changing the following:

- "I never win the big ones" TO _____

- "I can't concentrate" TO _____

- "I'm afraid I'll make a mistake" TO _____

- "I feel like dropping out" TO _____

- "I am too old and too slow" TO _____

What are some of your self-made traps of negativity? Write them out and immediately create the opposite. Negative thoughts are not blueprints nor etched in stone. Oftentimes these have no relation to reality.

- STATE WHAT YOU WANT: This guideline enables you to create an affirmation from a statement of your short-term goal. For example:

	Short-Term Goal		Affirmation
1.	To shed limiting beliefs	—	"I am willing to let go of self-limiting beliefs."
2.	To stop being self-critical	—	"I am a worthwhile, energetic athlete."
3.	To overcome fear of hills	—	"I love hills; they are my friends."
4.	To become less tense	—	"I become calmer every day in every way."
5.	To better cope with setbacks	—	"I view setbacks as opportunities for growth."
6.	To neutralize the opponent	—	"Calm and confident, I run well."

This works for long-term goals as well. Use this method for any of your desires, in sport or in your personal life.

HOW TO USE AFFIRMATIONS

These phrases can be used alone or together with visualization and imagery. Although they are most effective in a relaxed state, you can recite them under your breath while walking around or waiting for a bus. Try affirming in the shower or while looking in the mirror as you comb your hair; driving in your car is an excellent place to repeat your words of success. Some athletes have recorded their affirmations on tape to be played at convenient times. Writing or typing them and posting them in places that you attend to each day will prove to be very powerful.

If you really feel creative, try making up a song or chant using your favorite affirmations. Finally, try to incorporate them into your conversation by simply being positive toward others, bringing out their best. When you give in this way, people are more likely to respond in similar fashion and return the positive statements. In this case, there is no need for following the rules. Just keep it positive and direct. Be prepared to experience dramatic changes in your life.

A word of caution must be offered. If you are feeling particularly upset, depressed or negative, don't use affirmations to escape. If you do, it will simply repress those feelings only to see them float to the surface at a later time. Instead, view the feelings as warning signs indicating that something is not right and take action to ameliorate the problem. After so doing, introduce positive affirmations to build yourself back to a place of strength.

SOME USEFUL EXAMPLES

By now you are certainly ready to take off on your own affirmation journey. The following represent examples of typical affirmations for various athletes. The possibilities are unlimited.

1. Self-Image
   - I love and appreciate myself
   - Lean and trim I perform to win
   - I am a whole and complete athlete
2. Ability
   - Everyday in every way I run faster and faster
   - Calm and confident I run well
   - Effortlessly I glide like a tireless deer
3. Opponents
   - Good competitors force me to perform my best
   - My opponent is not important; I'm well trained
   - I am in control and ready to roll

4. Confidence
   - I improve with each move
   - I perform in good form above the norm
   - I may not win, but I'll run one hell of a race

5. Concentration
   - Focus now, focus now, focus now
   - I keep my mind on the task at hand
   - Distraction facilitates attention

6. Goals
   - I control the goal and go for the gold
   - Setbacks are opportunities that help me reach the goal
   - Expect success

7. Injuries
   - Healthier and stronger, longer and longer
   - My limber, flexible self restores itself to health
   - Health is me; I'm injury-free

One final word about affirmations. During my high school basketball days, I played against an incredible athlete from Rice High School in New York City. His name was Dean "the Dream" Memminger. He was truly a player that most coaches dream about having on their club. He dazzled thousands of fans in college and into the pros where he played for the New York Knicks. To watch him lead a fast break and shuffle the ball to the trailing teammate on the blind side, only to catch it back and stuff it with a 180° slam dunk, was like it really didn't happen—was I dreaming? That nickname conveyed a powerful image to me, yet somehow, I know it inspired Dean to respond with his best. Nicknames, like labels, tend to produce images which influence behavior. They are self-fulfilling prophecies. You see it happen to kids in school all the time: he's lazy, she's dumb; sure enough, they live up to the billing.

In athletes, such affirmations can work for you. College and university nicknames are specifically designed, not only to provide a mascot, but to be the source of inspiration and school spirit when possible: the Fighting Irish, the Bruins, the Running Rebels and the Mustangs are but a few. How about "Magic" Johnson, "Doctor J," "Silk," "Phi Slamma Jamma" or Earl "the Pearl"? Such tags clearly indicate something positive about those labeled as such. Give yourself a tag and experience it during your imagery. If self-conscious about it, keep it to yourself and sub-vocalize it whenever performance time arrives.

QUANTUM QUOTES

I have an expression that says, "One well-said quote is worth thousands of words." Quotes are words that create a broad picture—an image of what one is thinking; they convey a philosophy, so to speak, that could be talked about for hours. For athletes on the run, such brevity, clarity and succinctness is crucial. My reasons for introducing each chapter with a pertinent quote were many: they're fun to read; some give a sense of history; they sometimes capture the essence of a chapter and prepare you for what's ahead. But most of all, they provide an image to the central nervous system which, in turn, enables the body to follow that image. When those pictures are powerful and positive, they provide you with prior mental rehearsal for improving performance. Like affirmations, they are words and, as such, have an intense impact on our behavior.

I have been collecting quotes since my adolescent years. They helped me to believe in myself and gave me hope for achieving my goals. Whenever I doubted the possibility of a dream, there were always the brilliant minds from the past who were "willing" to lend their support. When confronting one's limitations and possibilities, encouragement to forge ahead is crucial. Remember the words of G.B. Shaw, "Some see things as they are and ask 'why?'; I dream of things that never were and ask 'why not?'" I consider this quote the most important set of words I've ever come across; for me, they gave me permission to expand what I once thought were limits. There are many people who are too willing to write dreams off as nonsense. You, too, must say "Why not?" to those cynics.

The following list presents a conglomeration of quotes I've gathered in the past, and others collected by a friend, Dr. Karl Mohr, whose work with athletes and optimal performance has been quite an inspiration to me.

The theme of these classic phrases is : You can do it! Use them to support your quest for excellence.

- There is only one thing that is powerful enough to make your life successful: YOU.
- What we intend happens and what happens is what we intend.

(George Leonard)

- Seldom do people or a team exceed their expectations.
- Whether you think you can or you think you can't, you are probably right.

(Henry Ford)

- What you can conceive and believe, you can achieve.

(Napoleon Hill)

- Expect success.
- What lies behind you and what lies before you are tiny matters compared to what lies within you.

(Emerson)

- Winning is an attitude.
- The greatest revolution in our generation is the discovery that human beings by changing the inner attitudes of their minds can change the outer aspects of their lives. Man alone of all the creatures on earth can change his own pattern. Man alone is the architect of his destiny.

(William James)

- There exists no thought in any mind but it quickly tends to convert itself into power.
- Man is an architect, the builder of himself.

(Emerson)

- As a man thinketh, so is he.
- You and I possess within ourselves, at every moment of our lives, under all circumstances, the power to transform the quality of our lives.

(Werner Erhard)

- Continually to strive is ultimately to become.
- Be ye transformed by the renewing of your minds.

(St Paul)

- To fly as fast as thought to anywhere that is, you must begin by knowing that you have already arrived.

(Chang)

- There is nothing that needs to be added to you in order for you to be an effective, successful and happy person. What seems important is to let go of any self-limiting thoughts or beliefs you have and allow creative and positive affirmations to assist you as you actively pursue your goals.

  (David Armistead)

- Your reach must exceed your grasp.

  (Robert Browning)

- The strength which holds you to your purpose in life is not your own strength, but the strength of the purpose itself, which is directly proportional to the importance you place in it.

- The mind is the limit. We know that it is not the body. As long as the mind can envision the fact that you can do something, you can do it—as long as you really believe 100 percent. It's all mind over matter.

  (Arnold Schwarzenegger)

- The body is the arrow; the will is the bow.

- The faculty of imagination is the great spring of human activity and the principal source of human improvement.

  (Dugald Stewart)

- Achievement is the inevitable and natural by-product of awareness.

  (Tim Gallwey)

- We are conditioned to believe that we can only learn so much so fast, that we are bound to be sick, that there are certain rigid limits to what we can do and achieve. We are bombarded constantly, from the day we are born, with limiting suggestions. Belief in limits creates limited people. Once people get over preconceived ideas about limitations, they can be much more.

  (Georgi Lozanov)

- We must create environments where people have permission to use their natural powers.

  (George Leonard)

- Both history and experimental data show that humans possess vastly larger capabilities than those they now use.

  (Georgi Lozanov)

- We are just beginning to discover the virtually limitless capacities of the mind.

  (Jean Houston)

- We will, by conscious command, evolve cerebral centers which will permit us to use powers that we now are not even capable of imagining.

  (Frederic Tilney)

- We are only now on the threshold of knowing the range of the educability of man—the perfectability of man. We have never addressed ourselves to this problem (extraordinary opportunity) before.

  (Jerome Bruner)

- We are hoarding potentials so great that they are just about unimaginable.

  (Jack Schwartz)

- I have learned there is no such thing any longer as a physical limit. It is the nature of the human animal to improve constantly. What I thought were limits have now been passed. If there is an end to what we can do, it is not within my comprehension.

  (Roger Counsil—coach of gymnast Kurt Thomas)

- To be a champion you must live like one.

- But do not pretend that people become great by doing great things. They do great things because they are great.

  (G. Bernard Shaw)

- Do you know what you are? You are a marvel. You are unique. In the millions of years that have passed, there has never been another child like you.

  (Pablo Casals)

- Argue for your limitations and sure enough, they're yours.

  (Richard Bach, author)

- In the realm of the mind, what you believe to be true is true.

  (John Lilly, M.D.)

- Man cannot discover new oceans unless he has the courage to lose sight of the shore.

  (Andre Gide)

- Beliefs are limits to be examined and transcended.
  (John Lilly, M.D.)
- A refined ability to tolerate and learn from failure and frustration is necessary to achieve excellence in any field.
- A human being alway acts, feels and performs in accordance with what he imagines to be true about himself and his environment.
  (Maxwell Maltz, M.D.)
- Our beliefs about ourselves and our world govern all our experience.
  (Adelaide Bry)
- When the imagination and the will are in conflict, the imagination invariably gains the day . . . the force of the imagination is in direct ratio to the square of the will.
  (Emile Coue)
- Man is not the sum of what he has already, but rather the sum of what he does not yet have, of what he could have.
  (Jean Paul Sartre)
- When I look back on all those worries, I remember the story about the old man on his death bed who said that he had a lot of trouble in his life, most of which never happened.
  (Winston Churchill)
- Man is what he believes.
  (Anton Chekhov)
- I have imagined and nothing that is real is alien to me.
  (G. Santayana)
- Compared to what we ought to be, we are only half awake. We are making use of only a small part of our physical and mental resources . . . the human individual thus lives far within his limits. He possesses power of various sorts which he habitually fails to use.
  (William James)
- The pain of living with yourself after a poor performance is much worse than the pain of the effort.
  (Tom Byers)
- AGE is mind over matter. If you don't mind, it doesn't matter.
  (Satchel Paige)

- When nothing seems to help, I go and look at a stonecutter hammering at his rock perhaps a hundred times without as much as a crack showing in it. Yet at the hundred and first blow it will split in two and I know it was not that blow that did it, but all that had gone before.

  (Jacob Riis)

- The most significant factor in running success is not the body . . . but the mind.

  (Marty Liquori)

- Sport demands an integration of the whole being. You can't be good in a sport unless you bring your emotions, mind, will and imagination into play.

  (Michael Murphy)

As a final word, I ask you to challenge yourself by creating a quote of your own. You can do it! You can do great things because you are great. I suggest keeping a journal of all thoughts that make sense to you; your own as well as those of others. As I conclude this chapter,

I am anticipating an 18-miler through the redwoods of the Santa Cruz mountains. Before this happens, I have a few words for myself:

> I love to run. I am in tremendous shape, physically and mentally. As I run, my mind and body are one. I have the power within me to make this run the most efficient, harmonious, enjoyable experience. I am a well-trained athlete.

> —*Jerry Lynch, 1985*

14

The mysical moment occurs as often as it does in sport in part because you don't have to have one. You are simply there to have a good time . . . when suddenly . . . it happens.

Michael Murphy

The Mystical with the Physical: Running and the Peak Experience

$\mathbf{N}$o book that concerns itself with optimal performance and mind-body phenomena would be complete if it overlooked the paranormal powers and extensional capabilities experienced by athletes. Inspired by Michael Murphy's and Rhea White's work, *The Psychic Side of Sports,* I decided to relate to you numerous extraordinary stories about runners who push themselves against the psycho-biological limits on the road to the "Peak Experience." Such an experience is a state of going beyond the ordinary; a sense of well-being where you feel tremendous surges of speed and power; the body gliding and floating effortlessly, over hilly terrain; a sense of unity with all that surrounds you; an incredible flash of confidence; a period of time where everything falls into place. Such moments of transcendence once were thought to be attainable only by powerful Eastern mystics with their extraordinary skills of concentration and meditation. Today, thousands of runners are discovering that their sport is the physical avenue to obtaining such mystical, ecstatic states. Reaching this level can be facilitated through top-level fitness, whatever that is. Not easily defined, a basic requirement for such fitness would be regular daily participation in a sport, aerobic in nature, for a period of 30 minutes or more. Mountain climbers, skydivers, skiers, parachutists and race car drivers would certainly qualify. Runners, for sure, make excellent use of their feet for such extraordinary feats.

A state of "going beyond" should not be confused with the release of beta endorphins commonly experienced after a grueling workout; that's a "runner's high." Peak experiences, although they may involve a release of such natural opiates from the brain, have a much broader scope. In their book, Murphy and White make it clear that when we push against our psycho-biological limits, the brain

213

tissues record a remarkable range of mystical pleasures: extraordinary inner vision, peace, stillness, calm, detachment, freedom, floating, ecstasy, power, control, immortality, unity, mystery and awe. These are but a few of the psychic rewards of sport, otherwise known as the peak experience.

The rewards of "going beyond" our psycho-biological limits have been experienced by athletes long before this country's love affair with distance running. Its roots originated well over 300 years ago with the mysticism of American Indian running traditions. Running to communicate, hunt and fight, these native Americans would cover hundreds of miles at a time and experience "wide open spaces" of their minds. While living in Boulder, Colorado in 1979, I met Bruce Gomez, a Pueblo Indian from Taos, New Mexico. We talked on a run one day about the transcendental nature of these extensive journeys on foot. The Indian runners would purposefully anticipate life-directing visions that would come to them on these dream-like sojourns. Visions of mountains moving and of voices of direction and advice were commonplace. A fascinating glimpse into the closed Pueblo world of Indian ritual and mysticism can be found in Peter Nabokov's work, *Indian Running*.

Psychiatrist Thaddeus Kostrubala has a sense of energy, pleasure and well-being following an extended run; fatigue is somehow strangely missing. In talking about the perfect shot, tennis champion Billie Jean King mentions how it usually happens when her concentration is perfect and the crowd is extremely enthusiastic. "It seems as though I'm able to transport myself beyond turmoil on the court to someplace of total peace and calm." I have often heard such experiences verbalized by runners who are able to create a sense of extreme detachment and a feeling of being in another world.

As a competitive runner who works with athletes and their mental training, you would expect me to be intrigued by such experiences. You are precisely right, although I did not connect my first few encounters with this phenomenon to the run itself. Instead, I attributed the emergence of such hidden reserves and capacities to some external occurrences beyond exercise. From my reading and talking with other runners about these extensional capabilities, I began to see the connection between the physical exertion and the extraordinary transformation of the mind. Since then, I make a habit of asking athletes to comment about times when they seem to have gone beyond what they thought possible; times when they ran "out of their bodies." What follows are excerpts of stories told to me by elite and recreational runners who were generous enough to invite me into their inner personal lives. Some are well-known; others less so. Interestingly enough, you'll discover that such experiences cut across all abilities to perform in an extraordinary way. We are all capable of "running to the peak."

The ability to perceive one's own internal anatomy is an experience often reported by distance runners. Michael Murphy refers to this as "inner seeing," a direct perception of structures such as organs, muscles and blood vessels. These athletes are not actually "seeing" their inner parts; it's simply a product of their imagination. Such stories are supported in fields outside of sport such as with those who practice yoga and meditation. Perhaps there are times while running when you feel some "tingling" in the extremities of your fingers. This happened to me when I first started running. It was as if I could "see" the blood pushing through to capillaries that had never been reached before. I envisioned my heart pumping so strongly that it forced the blood to explore territory previously unknown to my body. Such an experience has created within me a super-sensitivity and awareness of inner bodily functions.

One of the most impressive elite runners I have had the pleasure of working with is Jon Sinclair, the world's hottest roadracer in 1982. Jon is well aware of such phenomena. "I've given it much thought," states Sinclair when asked if he's experienced extensional peak moments. "I've never really thought of those types of feelings as unusual. I've had several occasions when everything clicked and I was running in, what seemed to be, greased grooves." He attributes it to "proper communication with my body." Jon also refers to this feeling as "gliding effortlessly" across the road. As I watched him "glide" on the beautiful tartan track at the Olympic Training Center, I couldn't help but think of how his stride was like a hydroplane, swiftly flowing above the surface. Poetry in motion. His movement mimicked the weightlessness experienced only by astronauts floating in a space capsule, defying all the laws of gravity. According to Sinclair, the feeling is one of "gliding without putting any energy into maintaining momentum." He attributes these occurrences to both strength and relaxation. "There is nothing magical about it nor can you have it all the time, either." He is quick to point out that speed, rather than being the root of pain, is a source of ecstasy that many runners overlook or misunderstand. Athletes, for years, have referred to ecstasy as the love of a struggle. The struggle and energy release from a good speed workout may very well prove ecstatic. Of his most difficult, struggling workouts, Sinclair states that, "They are the worst feelings in the world . . . and the best." One thing seems to be certain: from the expression on Jon's face, I feel as though I'm missing out on something. Where are my spikes?

Recently I had the chance to communicate with John Tuttle following his marvelous finish at the 1983 New York Marathon. What struck me about John as we worked together during the preceding summer was his almost childlike curiosity about the mental aspects of training. Like a "kid in a candy store," he wanted it all. His rapid breakthrough with marathoning is probably the result of this sponge-like quality, trying to absorb all that he can in order to improve. John mentioned how he was able to float along during the race, even with fatigue on his shoulders. "I had so much confidence . . . I was in control, able to move with anyone. I had seen this happening before it actually occurred, primarily during my visualization and workouts." Tuttle, truly running "out of his mind," experienced a sense of flying, lightness, power and control. He recounts how "At mile 16, I strained my hamstring, but I knew I would still finish . . . I was in complete control." There's no question about this as the rest is history. John ran a 2:10:51 in one of his finest efforts for the distance, setting a PR and finishing in fourth place.

Other runners have described similar personal experiences of flying, floating and weightlessness as they glide over the ground. Completely fatigued after 600 miles of running, Bill Emmerton explains how he had "this light feeling . . . as though I was going through space, treading on clouds." British marathoner Ian Thompson claims that "I only have to think about putting on my running shoes and the kinesthetic pleasure of floating starts to come over me."

On a different plane altogether is the adventuresome Chris Reveley, mountain runner and triathlete, par excellence. Winning the Pike's Peak Marathon for two consecutive years, in addition to three first-place finishes in the grueling Peak-to-Peak Triathalon, entitles Chris to such acclaim. Of course, there's his running up 22,834 foot Aconcagua in South America, a 50-mile roundtrip with a vertical elevation gain of 13,000 feet. Running volcanoes in Mexico and various peaks in the Himalayas are just part of his story. Quite unassuming, Chris underplays these accomplishments and focuses instead on the internal rewards—those feelings of ecstasy while stretching to the limits. The euphoria and exhilaration of the run, coupled with scaling massive rocks with a backdrop of nature's beauty, creates an ecstasy beyond description. A peak experience, indeed, literally and figuratively. Running-climbers often talk about their gratifying struggle against the natural elements; in addition to the ever-present danger where reality becomes a life/death issue, there is an emotional "rush" and overpowering joy attached to "coming out on top" of it all. Climber Lionel Terra scaled huge rocks because it "made me crazy with joy." According to Chris, "Confronting the difficulties and being able to function calmly in a high-stress situation, gives you the confidence to manage other difficult aspects of life." Confidence and inner control are some of the rewards for going beyond. Chris cautions, however, that some of his activities are unforgiving. You should learn to do it right before running with Chris up a mountain.

Another adventurer in search of ecstatic experiences through running is Gordon Jones, long time resident of that famous center of running, Boulder, Colorado. His extreme sense of euphoria is often experienced while running some of Colorado's numerous 14,000-foot peaks. He describes his descent of James Peak as if he were "out of his own body" looking at himself swiftly galloping over the rocks and between the trees in effortless fashion. He talks about the magic joy of what seemed to be a run that lasted for an entire year; this four-hour excursion included vast climatic changes of falling of snow at 14,280 feet, then hail, rain and warm 80° sunshine as he dropped through various elevation changes to 5,210 feet; running in Colorado in July is an experience to behold.

Dick Beardsley, one of this country's greatest marathoners, shared with me a brief, yet powerful, example of extensional capability. "Sometimes I will be out training and I get this unbelievable feeling through my body and mind. It's like I could run forever and

ever.'' Beardsley describes one of those rare moments when everything clicks. To him, the feeling occurs once or twice a year, yet
such intermittent reinforcement is a constant source of motivation for
Dick: ''Today may be the day I get that feeling.'' Incredible muscle
fluidity, a feeling of being suspended above the ground, almost as if
you were riding a horse, because the legs under you move so effortlessly. Beardsley reassures me that he's going to bottle it if he can.

Having had this experience yourself, how much would you be willing
to pay for such a potion? Perhaps I should pose this question to the
athletes who run the Western States 100.
    Then there is Dean Matthews, winner of the 1979 Honolulu
Marathon. A close friend of Beardsley, Dean believes that every
athlete strives for that ''peak experience''; it's something he does on
a daily basis. ''Such experiences are within all of us if we challenge
ourselves to explore them.'' Yet if we expend energy keeping them
from happening, they never will. One must be able to ''flow with the
tide.'' During the Honolulu Marathon, where he set the course record

and beat the likes of Shorter, Durden and Kardong, Matthews "felt like a fine-tuned racing machine that dared to be challenged. My breathing was rhythmic and as natural and easy as a leisurely walk. Each stride seemed to bounce and thrust forward without effort. Was this really me? It created a burst of incredible energy inside, one that I had never before experienced. I was into myself so intensely that I briefly remember catching the leader, Ron Tabb, and passing him with a surge never to look back. The feeling was one of efficient gliding. As the race progressed, each stride felt stronger and I became more confident. Something was really clicking for me that day that I can't explain. I experienced a sensation that I believe can only happen with hard work."

Athletes who push their limits often relate to experiencing an overwhelming sense of awe during peak moments. For example, a local "hot shot" surfer-runner from Santa Cruz, California, described his most recent high as "a never-ending experience. I thought I'd never come out of that tube." He managed to catch the perfect wave, staying in the curl for 15 seconds—considered quite a long time by these human seals. This story was retold to me on a run hours after the experience, yet its impact remained as if it had occurred seconds ago. He kept repeating, "I can't believe it; I can't believe it."

Along the same avenue, Dick Schaap recounts the 1968 Olympics and the story of Bob Beamon's extensional experience when he broke the world record in the long jump by almost 2 feet. According to Schaap, Beamon was awe-struck by his performance: "Tell me I'm not dreaming. It's not possible. I can't believe it. Tell me I'm not dreaming."

Pushing the psycho-biological limits of one's body is nothing new for Gary Morris, a California businessman and runner. After an unsuccessful attempt, Gary was triumphant in running 146 miles from Death Valley to the top of Mt. Whitney. In the contiguous United States, you can't get any lower or higher in terms of elevation change. Starting out at 272 feet below sea level, he battled rough terrain and drastic temperature changes from 20 F. to 118 F., finishing the sojourn at an elevation of 14,485 feet. Such variance in elevation, temperatures and terrain were paralleled by extreme fluctuations in his physical and emotional reactions, as well as a loss of

perspective of time, distance and equilibrium. But the denouement of these changes was an ultimate sense of peace and calm. The single-mindedness of Gary's goal became, in itself, a form of concentration which produced effects on his body beyond his wildest imagination. The final mile to the top was truly a "peak" experience. Gary relates how "All the systems which had served me so well, seemed to have gone crazy. Waves of emotion came crashing over me without warning. I was off-balance physically and emotionally. At times, a single step in the wrong direction meant a plunge of several thousand feet to my death. It was cold, icy and numbing to all my senses. More than once I passed into unconsciousness for a split second. The end seemed like an eternity. At 8:37 a.m. I arrived at the summit, 76 hours and 36 minutes after taking that first step. I cried more than a little."

Of the aforementioned stories, perhaps the most encompassing in terms of the number of psychic rewards are the experiences of marathoner-Triathlete Amy Haberman from California. She seems to agree with most reports that such rewards are the result of hard physical work of at least 30 minutes in duration. It takes that long, according to Amy, to feel a certain tempo as the body and mind work together. Talking about a training run, she describes how "the surface of the trail and the surrounding redwood giants begin to envelop me and the initial pain of pushing up the mountain begins to diminish. It's a freeing feeling as if I could go on forever."

In the *Psychic Side of Sports,* Michael Murphy refers to it as a feeling of release, known only in those moments when everything goes right. One of those moments came when David Henry set his 1968 Olympic record in the 400-meter hurdle. Like Amy, David felt that his mind and body worked almost as one: "My limbs reacted as my mind was thinking—total control, which resulted in absolute freedom." Amy also talks about her bursts of creativity while on a beautiful run. "Ideas kept flowing freely during this time of unusual creativity. I was out to play and take a break from struggling with writing a paper. I couldn't believe how the ideas kept coming and the pieces began to gel. A tremendous sense of clarity fell over me. I wrote that whole paper on the run. It was the easiest manuscript I've ever written. Don't ask me to explain it!"

Sensing her ease and openness with the subject, I asked Amy to recall any psychic rewards attached to competition. Naturally, she chose a race appropriately called, The World's Toughest Triathlon, in the mountains of Lake Tahoe. That's a 120-mile bike ride, a 2.4-mile swim in 58° F spine-chilling water, topped off with a grueling 26.6-mile run on relentless hills. With pain etched on her face, Amy recalled how "I started to get numb—my hands, arms, legs. I felt as if I were going to die. The feeling was one of complete detachment; I was out of my body and observing this person struggling to get to shore." Roger Bannister also felt this detachment halfway through the race that broke the four-minute mile. This feeling seems to be experienced by athletes who are totally self-involved in their events. Amy was definitely that involved according to her report. Even following a bout with hypothermia, she was able to jump on the bike and begin the vicious climb up Luther Pass, to an elevation of 7,746 feet. Reality became the moment-to-moment pushing of the pedals to get them to make one revolution after the other. At the top, she burst into tears. "It was a happiness I've never experienced. My heart burst open with a sense of extreme exhilaration. A feeling of un-forgettable peace, stillness, calm and joy set in. I was so alive—yet, an hour before, so close to death. I feel so fortunate to have experienced such a wide range of powerful feelings." Have you ever wondered why some are so willing to subject themselves to such dogged pursuits? After our talk, Amy suggested that I join her on a mountainous run of 25 miles in the morning. My answer was—only if it were preceded by a 120-mile bike ride. Without the slightest hesitation, she agreed. Uh, just kidding Amy! I think I'll detach myself from the pain before it begins.

It has been said that the famous German composer, Wolfgang Mozart was capable of "hearing" complex musical arrangements in his mind. Much of his brilliant music was written in a relaxed-meditative state. If running is the relaxed, meditative activity that people

claim it to be, is it any wonder that some of us experience melodies, rhythms and other forms of inner sound? Mick Jagger of the Rolling Stones runs up to 5 miles a day prior to an extended concert tour. He claims that it helps him to get in shape for what lies ahead. I wonder how many musical arrangements have come into focus during such exercise. A local Santa Cruz musician-runner claims that some of his best songs were conceived on the trails running through the mystical redwoods. He states that running seems to mimic a beat, cadence or rhythm; some have even compared it to a dance—"poetry in motion." I have often noticed how familiar tunes pop into my consciousness during an extended run through a forest; these musical "recordings" seem to be played perfectly in my mind as if I were listening to my home stereo sound system.

Perhaps you haven't experienced such psycho-biological phenomena; maybe you have, but failed to make the connection or have forgotten about it. One thing is certain; with an open mind and some hard workouts, the experiences are within reach. You don't need to have the physical abilities of the elite; a strong effort in a regular training run will do it. And understand that such experiences don't happen often but when they do you'll probably be aware of it from now on.

As I talk to runners, I begin to get the feeling that so many of us lose perspective as to why we are putting in the miles. We focus on faster times and winning prizes only to become frustrated when we fail to realize these goals. The purpose of this chapter is to encourage you to "go beyond and reach within" to experience the many rewards and pleasures running has to offer. Hopefully this will motivate you to "stick with it" when your running seems to be going nowhere. The only ingredient necessary for extensional capability is an open mind and hard work. The next time you stand at the starting line or go out for a training run, remember that this could be the time when you truly reach the peak. It's wise to carry a dollar bill in your running shorts at all times. Rather than interrupt such an event, you will want to call someone after the run to say you'll be a little late for dinner.

Index

227